Embodied Cross

Embodied Cross

Intercontextual Reading of *Theologia Crucis*

ARATA MIYAMOTO

WIPF & STOCK · Eugene, Oregon

EMBODIED CROSS
Intercontextual Reading of *Theologia Crucis*

Copyright © 2010 Arata Miyamoto. All rights reserved. Except for brief quotations in critical publications or reviews, no part of this book may be reproduced in any manner without prior written permission from the publisher. Write: Permissions, Wipf and Stock Publishers, 199 W. 8th Ave., Suite 3, Eugene, OR 97401.

Wipf & Stock
An Imprint of Wipf and Stock Publishers
199 W. 8th Ave., Suite 3
Eugene, OR 97401
www.wipfandstock.com

ISBN 13: 978-1-60899-149-5

Manufactured in the U.S.A.

All scripture quotations, unless otherwise indicated, are taken from the Holy Bible, New International Version®, NIV®. Copyright ©1973, 1978, 1984 by Biblica, Inc.™ Used by permission of Zondervan. All rights reserved worldwide.

Contents

Acknowledgments vii
Introduction ix

1 Luther and Orthopraxis 1

2 God in Context 32

3 Buddhism and Theology of the Cross 66

4 Theology without the Cross 85

5 A Theology of the Cross in Encounter with Cosmic *Dukkha* 115

Bibliography 141

Acknowledgments

This book is based on my dissertation submitted to the Lutheran School of Theology at Chicago in 2009. The entire dissertation project was made possible because of the partnership between the Japanese Evangelical Lutheran Church and the Evangelical Lutheran Church in America. The Global Mission Unit of the Evangelical Lutheran Church in America provided me with a global fellowship, including a generous scholarship. My stay in Chicago has also been a great period of time to learn about the ELCA's historical commitment to missionary work in Japan. Recognition of this fact, for which I am thankful, came to me through acquaintances with people like Franklin Ishida (the former director for International Leadership Development); Tammy Jackson (the present director for International Leadership Development); and innumerable congregation members who have showed me and my family hospitality. I am grateful for the sisters and brothers of my church, the Japan Evangelical Lutheran Church. Yoshiro Ishida, Naozumi Eto, and George Oshiba encouraged me to come out of my local context and to study at the Lutheran School of Theology at Chicago.

Second, I must acknowledge my professors who led me to the challenging subject of theology. The academic setting of Hyde Park, Chicago, within and out of LSTC, is overwhelming and astonishing. This amazing academic setting provided me with an opportunity to open myself to ecumenical and interdisciplinary realms through my professors' instruction, lectures, and conversations. These professors included: Theodore W. Jennings Jr. (Chicago Theological Seminary); Hans Joas (the Committee on Social Thought at the University of Chicago); Robert Schreiter (Catholic Theological Union); William Schweiker (Divinity School at the University of Chicago); and Bo Myung Seo (Chicago Theological Seminary). It was my professors at the Lutheran School of Theology at Chicago who pushed me to deeply consider my faith tradition in this circumstance. Mark Thomsen and Vitor Westhelle gave me a great deal of theological insight and guided me to take up theology of the cross as my dissertation topic. Linda Thomas and Antje Jackelén led me to a firm conviction that theology not remain an ivory tower and that it can be theology only when theology is done in the living context of human beings. Paul Chung at Luther Seminary showed generous guidance, which enabled me to address my cultural background in the project more seriously. Notwithstanding all these wonderful opportunities, I could not have completed my project without the consistent mentoring of Jose David Rodriguez. The academic journey with him was itself intercontextual. It led me to open my eyes to a more complicated and varied reality of my life with others. Finally, I express my appreciation for Rob Worley, director of Language Resource Writing Center. His Arabic coffee gave me the best way of breathing fresh air.

After the completion of my doctoral study, I went back to a ministry in Japan. My congregation, Hakata Lutheran Church in Fukuoka City, convinced me about the origin of theological insight. I wish to thank many people, including my colleagues and members from my church, who offered valuable evaluations and critiques of the material in this book. I especially wish to thank Kenneth Dale-sensei who gave me a great deal of encouragement to keep going.

Most of all, I am thankful for my family. My parents are the ones most pleased with the completion of my project. Their faithful dedication their mission in Japan has encouraged me to accomplish the project as my calling. The completion of this project also could not have happened without the companionship of my wife, Saori. Her brightness, patience, and sociability are nothing less than gifts to me. For my daughter, Hana, who came to Chicago at six months old, Hyde Park is like her home. Her existence, along with her little brother Narumi (who joined us soon after our return to Japan) has made the quality of my life different. I appreciate all these gifts I have been given.

Introduction

THIS BOOK FIRST AIMS to outline an intercontextual reading of a theology of the cross (*theologia crucis*) that flows across a global context.[1] A theology of the cross functions to advance the question of revelation in different times and space (i.e., the revelation of the divine presence on the cross of Jesus Christ). This revelation is decisive for humanity, not merely because of the content but also because of the disposition of the revelation. It influences our attitudes for life. Through this project, I propose a theology of the cross that enables theologians to address divine self-revelation *on* and *from* the cross and do theology *within* and *beyond* religious-cultural boundaries.

The method guiding this intercontextual theology of the cross is based on a contextual theological approach.[2] Contextual theology is a relatively recent theological movement, beginning in the 1960s and 1970s, launched in multiple regions to develop theologies of struggle with and for the marginalized, the poor, and the oppressed.[3] From the beginning, it has paralleled liberation theology in a broader sense. However, shortly,

---

1. *Theologia crucis* is rooted in Luther's early works, but I primarily explore contemporary theologians who take Luther's contributions to their constructive theological proposals seriously. From this perspective, the theology of the cross does not primarily designate a particular theological discourse *about* the cross. Rather, it means the particular disposition of a theologian (Christian) who starts doing theology from the foot of the cross. The theology of the cross connects to the conviction that the cross is where God revealed himself in a unique way.

2. My basic understanding of contextual theology is framed by Robert Schreiter and Stephen Bevans, who originally proposed this theological method in their writings. See Schreiter, *Constructing Local Theologies*; Bevans, *Models of Contextual Theology*.

3. See Gutierrez, *Theology of Liberation*; Cone, *Black Theology of Liberation*; Cone, *God of the Oppressed*; Moltmann, *Crucified God*. The term contextual theology was refined by the Theological Education Fund in 1972: "Contextualization includes all that is implied in the other terms *indigenization* and *inculturation*, but seeks also to include the realities of contemporary secularity, technology, and the struggle for human justice." In Bevans, *Models of Contextual Theology*, 26, quoting from Theological Education Fund, *Ministry in Context*.

some began to recognize that liberation theology brought something crucial beyond their particular contexts.[4] While liberation theologians broke through the conventional theological tendency for universalism, they also opened a path toward Christian tradition in a different way.[5] In short, they provided a new way of doing theology. With this awareness, Stephan Bevans proposes his thesis, "Contextualization is a theological imperative,"[6] and summaries the revolutionary changes in theological method when compared with "classical theology."

First, contextual theology stands for a theological approach that is aware of the fact that theological reflection cannot ignore human experience, whether personal or collective, whether past or present, and whether social or cultural. Second, in order to consider experience, contextual theologians think that knowledge is deeply embedded in the social-cultural matrix.[7] They presuppose the idea that Scripture and tradition are also the accumulation of knowledge based on past contextual experiences. Third, I will intentionally try to maintain this contextual approach following these three principles: 1) contextual theology develops in a missional context; 2) contextual theology is plural; 3) the nature of contextual theology is inclusive, not exclusive. Finally, as a consequence, these insights lead contextual theology to a dialogical approach to Christian traditions.

Contextual theology is not exclusive to Christian tradition. Rather, it places itself in a dialogical relationship with the diverse resources found in the tradition. All these elements of contextual theology that Schreiter and Bevans present clearly propose a methodology to advance contextual theology in order for local churches to engage in constructing theology in their own way while sustaining a deep connection to tradition. However, while they enhance the possibility of contextual theology within the framework of catholicity, it remains under the larger question of how a contextual theology engages in dialogue with other contextual theologies by recognizing difference as difference. In other words, how

---

4. See Bosch, *Transforming Mission*, 432–47; Bevans and Schroeder, *Constants in Context*, 305–22.

5. Schreiter proposes a new way of approaching tradition in the process of constructing a local theology, in *Constructing Local Theologies*, 95–121.

6. Bevans, *Models of Contextual Theology*, 15.

7. Ibid., 3–7.

does a contextual theology open itself to others?[8] This is the reason that contextual theology necessitates an intercontextual perspective. Noting that any theology has its own perspective, I would like to assert sensitively the value of plurality among contextual theologies. But instead of asserting *sameness*, I will seek a common place to engage them. I believe that contextual theology as a theological method requires that I seek a common ground for conversation without distorting the reality of plurality, if it enhances the capacity for intercontextual dialogue with other contextual theologies.

Ten years after Schreiter's seminal work in contextual theology, *Constructing Local Theologies*, was published, he revised some crucial points in terms of his understanding of culture.[9] In his previous work, in order to elevate the importance of culture for local theology, he proposed the semiotics of culture. In this work, culture tended to remain a static and independent entity, but in *The New Catholicity*, Schreiter offers a deeper perspective of cultural study derived from postcolonial criticism: power relations in terms of culture. The amendment is aimed at paying attention to the complicated web of realities within and without one's culture. He reflects the postcolonial approach as he says: "Culture strives to establish a 'third place' between self and other, beyond colonizer and colonized."[10] What he means is that identity, whether Christian or cultural, is "multi-layered and hybridized." Schreiter develops this element of cultural study into a theological method based on the theory of intercultural hermeneutics.

He defines intercultural hermeneutics as a communication theory to "make communication possible across cultural boundaries."[11] Introducing intercultural hermeneutics into the methodology of contextual theology helps one take the multiplicity of epistemology into account: the multiplicity of meaning, truth, and agency.[12] The merit of

---

8. Kristeen Kim names the weakness of contextual theology: "Theology in one context cannot be challenged by outsiders to that context." In saying so, she expresses her concern about a criterion for contextual theologies, as she says: "If theology done in a particular context has no awareness of global concerns or interest in the theologies of others, it risks the parochialism that Missiology inherently challenges." In Kim, "Missiology as Global Conversation," 47–48.

9. Schreiter, *New Catholicity*, 57–61.

10. Ibid., 54.

11. Ibid., 28.

12. Ibid., 39–44.

intercultural theology invites us into the dynamic process of dialogue in the "third place." It makes it possible to open the gap between one static theological view and the other side of the theology. It is good at addressing other as other, different as different. It avoids the essentialism and substantialism of contextual elements. It also avoids universalizing and objectifying one point of view. Rather, the dialogue stimulates the third place and seeks the whole picture through the dialogue. This point is my aim to introduce an intercontextual reading. I will pay attention to a multiplicity of context rather than single context.

In the opening chapter, I will explore three theologians in North America: Mark Thomsen, Mary Solberg, and Vitor Westhelle. Each offers a fine example of practicing an intercontextual theology of the cross. Mark Thomsen constructs his theology of the cross in the intersection of North America with the third world from the perspective of global missiology. He clarifies the transition of a theological issue from the reality of sin to the reality of absurd suffering in terms of the theology of the cross. Mary Solberg practices the theology of the cross to challenge a dominant system of knowing/knowledge that claims its own objectivity and absoluteness. She presents the "epistemology of the cross" in her multiple conversations with feminist epistemologies and Luther's theology of the cross. Her theology of the cross lifts up the importance of everyday experiences and eventually comes to the proposal of "strategic objectivity."

Finally, Vitor Westhelle proposes a fundamental question that any discourse, any theology in particular, must address: the "epistemic key." He radicalizes theology to the point where a theologian pushes him or herself to the borders of language, knowledge, and discourse. This makes us open ourselves to others. Their contextual theologies of the cross are firmly grounded on Luther's theology of the cross. They prove that contextual theology does not necessarily take an exclusive position within Christian tradition. Rather, they shed new light on Luther's theology: a theology of the cross as orthopraxis. The orthopraxis of Luther's theology of the cross helps them not only develop their contextual reflection on Christian faith but also restores the tradition of liberation traced in the church fathers. A contextual theology of the cross can be functional in order for one to practice an intercontextual reading of the cross across multicontextual borders.

In the following three chapters, I will focus on a theology of the cross in a Japanese context. Japanese theologian Kazoh Kitamori published *Theology of the Pain of God* in Japan in 1946 just after World War II. The thesis at the center of his theology is that the heart of the gospel is the pain of God. He is the initiator who tries to synthesize Luther's theology of the cross with the Japanese sensibility of *tsurasa* (bitter feeling). I will explore the theology of the pain of God in light of contextual theology in chapter 2. It necessarily leads me to reread the theology of the pain of God from the intercontextual perspective. I will practice it by focusing on two perspectives. One is his religious-cultural perspective in terms of the view of God. Kitamori opened a way to do theology by which a theologian takes his or her religious-cultural tradition seriously. It is noteworthy that he introduced aesthetic language into the doctrine of God. On the other hand, when his text is transferred to other contexts, it illumines other contextual issues that this theology retains. I will explore the theology of the pain of God in the Asian context through conversation with other Asian theologians of the cross. In this section, I will present not only the contribution of Kitamori's theology but also issues that his theology raises across a context.

One of most crucial theological issues in Asia, and in Japan in particular, is how to approach the diverse religiosity in Asia. Especially in East Asia, Buddhism is foundational for people's way of life. In inverse proportion to the long history of Buddhism, the history of Christian engagement in Buddhism is not so long. In chapter 3, I will summarize the interfaith dialogue between Christianity and Buddhism through the dialogue between Abe Masao, a Japanese Buddhist scholar, and Western theologians. Interestingly, Abe proposes a Buddhist interpretation of a theology of the cross in order to seek common ground with a Christian understanding of God. While leading theologians who focus on a theology of the cross sincerely engage in dialogue with him, they also question Buddhist understanding of history and ethics through their conversations, which makes the dialogue richer for my intercontextual project. This chapter also prepares the reader for the exploration of Asian theology of the cross in chapters 4 and 5.

Yagi Seiichi is one of the pioneers who opened a mutual understanding between Christianity and Buddhism. He shares the same hope with Abe in that he believes Christian faith can be transformative through engagement in interfaith dialogue. I will explore how a Christian in a Buddhist context reflects on a theology of the cross through the study of Yagi's theology. While Yagi recognizes how different the religions of Christianity and Buddhism are, he tries to find a common ground between them. While learning the Buddhist understanding of suffering (cosmic *dukkha*), he came to realize the cause of suffering from his own ego in a Buddhist manner. The causality of the ego cannot be merely reduced to one's own individuality. Yagi is also aware that the human ego is a socio-cultural product nurtured by its language/knowledge system. Thus, liberation from the ego bound to the system of knowledge should be sought to awaken the true self. As a result, he proposes the "ego awakened to the Self/Christ" as the most fundamental experience of conversion in the New Testament.

Both Abe and Yagi focus on the individual or existential solution of the cosmic dukkha in the tradition of Buddhism. In the encounter with Buddhism, Yagi provides a unique notion of faith and liberation. By the same token, he presents a new way of talking about God in the Japanese-Buddhist context. On the other hand, by seeking an individual-existential solution to suffering, a theology of the cross disappears in his theology. It is more controversial in a broader context of a theology of the cross that the cosmic dimension of suffering is reduced to the existential solution. This is the more intensive concern of other Asian theologians. I will shift my focus to the Korean theologian Paul Chung in order to disclose the comprehensive theology of the cross in an Asian-Buddhist context in chapter 5.

Paul Chung is a unique theologian in the sense that he pursues the "irregular grace of God" in the Asian double contextual arena of "poverty" and "religious plurality."[13] He presents a comprehensive theology of the cross, as he says, "Asian theology of the cross pursues divine suffering in personal, social, political, cosmological realms and also in multi-religious dimension."[14] The three dimensions of suffering are not exclusive to each other but integrate the complex human reality of suffering. While developing an interreligious hermeneutics, Chung contextualizes Luther's theology of the cross in the Asian context, and in doing

13. He argues that an "irregular theology" in a Lutheran sense makes it possible to deal with "unmethodical, chaotic, and provocative dimensions in the deliberation of the Word of God," in his article: "Lutheran Theology in Engagement with World Religions," 336. In his latest writings, he fully develops his "Asian irregular theology," which makes it possible to reflect more constructively and critically on the irregularity of God's Word in action in encounter with Asian massive suffering (*minjung*) and the life-world of East Asian religions. See Chung, *Christian Mission*; Chung, *Karl Barth*.

14. Chung, *Martin Luther and Buddhism*, 188.

so, he finds a lead to the cosmic Christology in Luther. The driving key to cosmic Christology is Luther's radical use of the doctrine of *communicatio idiomatum*. Luther's early work tends to emphasize the historical Jesus, but his later works on sacramental theology cling more to the ubiquitous and real presence of Christ on a universal scale. However, Chung never separates the cosmic Christ from the historical cross of Jesus. He integrates the crucified Christ into the cosmic Christ. This recognition of the co-suffering of the humanity of Jesus and the divinity of Christ is captured in this sentence: "God's unselfish cosmic love encounters the cosmological *dukkha* in all sentient creatures."[15] In developing Luther's theology of the cross in the encounter with the cosmic dukkha, he comprehensively integrates the cosmic Christ with Christ as liberator, which is part of his contextual background of Korean *minjung* theology. Through an intercontextual reading of the cross, Chung presents a radical understanding of the gospel from the perspective of the cross. After I explore Chung's comprehensive theology of the cross, I will offer a concluding argument for this research.

A theology of the cross is more than a theology *about* the cross, such as atonement theories. I do not intend to make a new theory or a doctrinal accumulation of thinking about the cross in this book. Rather, my concern is to explore the niche between the event and discourse that a theology of the cross brings about by focusing on more methodological issues in terms of contextual theology. However, I will show that a theology of the cross does not allow me even to identify it with a methodology. It is an unmethodological method and a disposition toward doing theology. It is certain that a theology of the cross starts with the recognition that Christian faith cannot avoid the historical event of the cross of Jesus. A theology of the cross carries the polarizing memories of the cross. One memory is of the terrible violence imposed on Jesus and the other is the memory of faith in the midst of the deepest abyss in human history. A theology of the cross contextualizes the dangerous combination of these memories in the present reality of life and death among us. Eventually, a theology of the cross is thoroughly preoccupied with the agency of God but not in a way that deals with the systematic apologetics of the knowledge of God. Rather, it deals with the knowledge of God before it becomes knowledge. It is the matter of the living and dying of our lives.

---

15. Ibid., 188.

1

Luther and Orthopraxis

OVERVIEW OF LUTHER'S THEOLOGY OF THE CROSS IN THE TWENTIETH CENTURY

Theologia Crucis as a Principle of the Knowledge of God

WALTHER V. LOEWENICH, A German theologian, returned Luther's theology of the cross to the forefront of twentieth-century theology by saying, "The theology of the cross is a principle of Luther's entire theology."[1] He reread the theology of the cross, which had been dealt with as a monkish remnant of Luther, as a theological principle of knowledge. In Loewenich's context, during a socio-political crisis in Germany in the beginning of the twentieth century, Luther's theology of the cross functioned to sharpen the discontinuity between God and human beings. Like Paul did in his theology of the cross (1 Cor 1:18), Loewenich presented it as a theology of revelation from the cross, saying:

> The cross opened up a completely new understanding of God . . . the knowledge of God and the word of the cross moved into the closest relationship. . . . God can manifest his wisdom only in foolishness. . . . God reveals himself in concealment, God's wisdom appears to men as foolishness, God's power is perfected in weakness, God's glory parades in lowliness, God's life becomes effective in the death of his Son . . . this means, furthermore, that a direct knowledge of God is impossible for man.[2]

1. Loewenich, *Luther's Theology*, 13.
2. Ibid., 11–12.

This revelation is full of paradoxes. God's wisdom takes in the foolishness and weakness of the cross. It is revelation but not like an epiphany in a general sense. The self-manifestation of God is indirect in the cross and suffering. It is a matter of faith whether we come to know God, not a matter of human reason or natural knowledge. Loewenich's proposal became foundational for subsequent discussions about a theology of the cross.

In the North American Lutheran context, Gerhard Forde emphasizes Luther's theology of the cross as the proclamation of the word of the cross by emphasizing the transformative event between "almighty" human beings and almighty God.[3] Like other orthodox Lutheran theologians who focus on the proclamation of the cross, Forde presents a theology of the cross as divine work that brings sinners to righteousness in terms of reconciliation. Suffering is not physical but spiritual, and the divine wrath lays it down on sinners. This focus on spiritual suffering seeks to represent Luther's passion for justification by faith in a contemporary context. Therefore, suffering is understood in the light of the doctrine of sin against a righteous God, which illustrates the basic human condition of seeking a way to follow the law of God by oneself.[4] Luther, Forde argues, recognizes that both his suffering and the cross of Jesus come from the wrath of God, because this wrath results from the violation of the law.

This theology of the cross connects the reality of suffering with sin, the wrath of God, and the forgiveness of sin. Forde seems to be representative of a Lutheran orthodox understanding of the cross, against which Mark Thomsen paints a different picture of a theology of the cross in an alternative framework. A point that divides these Lutheran scholars is the way of perceiving the reality of suffering in the light of the cross.[5] Reflecting on the massive suffering of people on a global scale, the more intense connection between suffering and a theology of the cross arises from those who grapple with social injustice.

---

3. Forde, *On Being a Theologian*.

4. Ibid., 27.

5. Douglas John Hall presents a theology of the cross in the North American context. Counting on his diagnoses like "triumphalism of Christianity" and "optimistic resurrectionism" in North America, Forde's theology of the cross may be reread as a contextual theology. See Hall, *Cross in Our Context*.

Voice from the Marginalized

The authors in the collection of essays *The Scandal of a Crucified World* show a decisive change in the theological paradigm in terms of suffering.[6] Yacob Tesfai, the editor of this book, summarizes this change in six remarks. First, whatever the interpretation of suffering and the cross in the Western Christian tradition, those who received the Christian symbol of the cross in the third world received the cross not as the symbol but as the representation of conquering and violence of their own land, birth, and culture. Second, traditional understandings like satisfaction and reconciliation are enslaved by the heaven complex as if they are able to talk about something from heaven. Third, the traditional understanding of the cross, which spiritualizes the cross of Jesus, distorts the crucial message of the cross: Jesus's life, ministry, and his consequential death; his poverty and homelessness; his subversive ministry against religious and political leaders; and his preference for the poor, oppressed, and marginalized. The cross is the result of his solidarity with the marginalized.

Fourth, the suffering and death of millions of people stimulate this authentic result of Jesus's ministry: his solidarity with people. Their lives and sufferings bring the epistemology of Jesus and God. For these people, the cross has an epistemological function. Fifth, in this sense, Jesus's cross is not merely a past event, but it designates the present cross-reality in this world. Jesus's cross and people's crosses are the consequence of the negation of the "God-given destiny of people."[7] Finally, the cross does not exist without resurrection, and vice versa. The resurrection is God's negation of human negation. The people in the margins make us look into the embodied suffering of the cross and the crosses there and here.

Interestingly, the period when contextual theology began to be taken seriously corresponds with the emergence of these critical voices in terms of a theology of the cross. The human reality of suffering is mutual to the understanding of the cross. The Lutheran traditional understanding of the cross, which is bound to the atonement theory, has been also challenged by these liberation perspectives of the suffering of the poor, the oppressed, and the marginalized. Their proposal is not confined to their ethical warning. It includes an agenda for a new intellectual approach to suffering. What is at stake is not how a conventional

---

6. Tesfai, *Scandal of a Crucified World*.
7. Ibid., 13.

theology approaches the cross but how the cross transforms the way of doing theology. Walter Altmann is the one who rereads Luther's theology of the cross from the perspective of liberation theology in the Latin American context.[8]

Despite the fact that the Latin American context is different from Luther's context, Altmann finds a series of commonalities between Luther and liberation theology by focusing on Luther's confrontation against the "deification of humanity and against the hierarchical and institutional system of the church."[9] The protest movement theologically converges on Luther's insight into Christ's being present with people. This Christ connects the suffering of Jesus with the suffering of modern people toward liberation through faith. The faith that Altmann learned from Luther is not an abstract Christological formula but a faith anchored in a concrete historical place where people met Jesus Christ. Faith in Christ is grounded in the "present reality of Christ." The Christology points to the correlation between divinity and humanity in Jesus Christ. From the conviction of this correlation, Luther's unique soteriology appears as a "happy exchange" between Christ and Christians. The provisional sign of the new life is not glory but the cross, but the present Christ encourages a move toward eschatological hope in believers.

According to Altmann, Luther abandons the medieval figure of the imitation of Christ. Instead, Luther proposes "conformation with Christ." The term in Latin, *conformitas*, has nothing to do with "conformity" in the English translation. It means becoming "con-formed" with Christ. "Through the happy exchange between Christ and the person who believes in Christ the believer becomes fused, or attached, to Christ and is led by Christ to a new life."[10] Altmann's rereading of Luther shows the liberation perspective in Luther's theology. He finds in Luther the "solidarity Christology" that encourages people to see their suffering as it is, to confront injustice, and to seek solidarity with others working toward liberation.

The three North American theologians I will take up in the following sections are deeply connected to these emerging voices coming from their own contexts. Vitor Westhelle originally comes from Brazil. Mary Solberg started her reflection of ethical epistemology from her experiences while

---

8. He is a contributor to *Scandal of a Crucified World* in chapter 6.
9. Altmann, *Luther and Liberation*.
10. Ibid., 21.

living in El Salvador. Mark Thomsen, though he originally worked as missionary in Africa, developed his global perspective from liberation theology like that of John Sobrino. All of them develop a unique insight into Luther's theology of the cross in their own theological contexts, but what they are in absolute concord with is the presence of Christ being tied with suffering people. Just as Altmann says, it is anchored both in liberation theology and in Luther. All consider that the presence of Christ involves suffering. Suffering is not merely a topic in ethics; rather it is an indispensable element that connects theology with one's own life, suffering, and world. However, just as contextual theology is not a new invention today, what liberation theology emphasizes is also not new. Conversely, the radical element of liberation theology sheds light on Christian tradition likely to be forgotten. In this sense, viewing the three theologians as contextual theologians also makes it possible to view them in light of Christian tradition with a new lens. Luther, liberation theology, and the three theologians in the North American context all share the same tradition that can be traced back to the church fathers. That is the type C that Justo González proposes in his historical study of Christian tradition.

Rethinking Christian Tradition in Light of the Theology of the Cross

Justo González presents a typology that presents three types of Christian thought and suggests type C has potential for twenty-first-century theological thought.[11] According to González, the Western theological tradition has been driven by type A, whose main category is "law" represented by Tertullian, and type B, whose main category is "truth" represented by Origen of Alexandria. However, he proposes type C as the one that has been almost left behind in Christian tradition in the West and whose concern is directed into the pastoral-historical matter represented by Irenaeus. However thin the tradition of type C is, it is not extinct from Christian tradition. In fact, González finds the reemergence of type C in the twentieth century in Karl Barth's theology, Lutheran theology in Sweden, the liturgical renewal in the Second Vatican Council, and liberation theology.[12] Regarding Luther's theology, he discovers a mixture of type A and type C. Lundensian Lutherans rediscovered this element in Luther.[13]

---

11. González, *Christian Thought*.
12. Ibid., 123.
13. Gustaf Aulén is a representative of Lundensian Lutherans and discovers Luther's

González argues that, although the forgiveness of sin, Luther's main concern, is dominant in type A, Luther also sustains and develops type C in his sacramental theology and Christology by emphasizing the presence of Christ in the Eucharist. Unlike type A, which understands sin legalistically, type C understands sin as a condition of being subject to Satan. Thus, salvation is not forgiveness but liberation from the power of Satan by Christ as liberator. Christ is incarnated in flesh and recapitulates and finally overcomes the fate of humanity captured by evil power. Salvation is implemented by believers who participate in the death and resurrection of Christ. It relies on the present reality of Christ. As Irenaeus shows, type C presents salvation in the history of salvation from the incarnation through the resurrection to eschatological consummation. González argues that the rediscovery of type C theology may well "provide the church at large with unexpected possibilities, and even open the way to new (and the rediscovery of ancient) understandings of catholicity and Christian unity."[14] I will explore the theologies of the cross that Thomsen, Solberg, and Westhelle present as those compatible with type C, as well as focusing on contextual theology by nature.

They are not liberation theologians in the strict sense of liberation theology. However, they show the applicability of liberation theology in a global context beyond the regional setting of liberation theology. I call their perspective a "liberative perspective" to distinguish it from liberation theology. Regarding the model of contextual theology that Bevans proposes, all of them attempt to develop Luther's theology of the cross from the perspective of the "praxis model."[15] The "North American Context" that I take into consideration is not a closed context demarcated by national or geographical boundaries. Their theological feature shows an interconnection with other contexts, like South America, the German-Protestant tradition, a global missiological context, and so on. A context cannot exist alone. Thus, I will emphasize the inter-contextual reading in each section. All three theologians clearly develop their own theological perspectives with this awareness. I would like to put them in a broader picture of Christian thought today.

---

elements of type C (classical model). Aulén, *Christus Victor*.

14. González, *Christian Thought*, 123.

15. See chapter 6 of *Models of Contextual Theology*, by Bevans. I prefer *orthopraxis* rather than *praxis* in order to indicate their theological perspective because of my focus on the aspect of their intellectual labor.

CRUCIFORMED *MISSIO DEI*: MARK THOMSEN

A theology of the cross has the potential for constructing a dynamic foundation for a contemporary vision of *missio dei*. Mark Thomsen attempts to propose a theology of the cross that takes the global context of the twenty-first century seriously from a Lutheran perspective. In doing so, the theology of the cross addresses new perspectives that Christianity faces: "A twenty-first century theology of the cross must be reconstructed to address the world of religious pluralism and the tragic identification of the cross with Western Christendom and imperialism."[16] While he positively appreciates that Lutheran missiological themes are rooted in biblical theology, he also recognizes the contextual and theological distance between the sixteenth-century Reformation in German and the twentieth-century global context. Like Luther, he starts his theology of the cross by focusing on a theology of revelation, but he expands its perspective from Luther's personal experience of justification by faith into the eschatological movement of *missio dei*. The theology of the cross enables us to participate in *missio dei* in this established global world where the reality of tremendous suffering is hidden in the theology of glory. He does not reduce the theology of the cross merely to a kind of atonement theory or theological program or one of doctrine. Rather, it is "the primary key for interpreting the whole of Christian thought and praxis."[17]

Conversation with Luther

Thomsen mainly takes up three aspects of Luther's theological heritage in considering the contextual theology of the cross. He believes that Luther's theology helps contemporary Christians construct a missiology in the broken web of the world. First, Luther seriously recognized the brokenness of humanity in relation to God. Justification by faith designates that God loves the world and all sinners, not because of their own efforts, but because of God's grace. Salvation is a gift from God. Second, Thomsen receives an insight from Luther's doctrine of the priesthood of all believers. In this theology, Luther declined the medieval Roman Catholic hierarchical ecclesiology, in which the Pope took responsibility

---

16. Thomsen, *Christ Crucified*, 39. He concretely takes up four theological locations to be addressed: 1) Religious pluralism; 2) imperial conflation of Christianity; 3) global divide; and 4) social evil: racism and sexism, materialism, triumphalism.

17. Ibid., 22.

for mission. The shift from a single authority for mission to an egalitarian distribution of responsibility is important to do the cruciformed *missio dei* in global context. While the church is primarily understood as a congregation—community of saints—not an institutional church, missiology should not be constructed from a single place to others but should be a multi-centered missiology practiced by congregations. It makes it possible to focus on local needs in the sense of mission. The theology of the cross is foundational in that believers think about the cruciformed mission in their own contexts. Even if it is brokenness and sinful reality that we see in each other, we can see goodness, love, and beauty in the midst of the evil, weakness, and brokenness through faith. It becomes clear that this radical worldview is grounded on Luther's theology of the cross, when he says: "sinners are attractive because they are loved; they are not loved because they are attractive. For this reason the love of man avoids sinners and evil persons . . . This is love of the cross, born of the cross."[18] The connection between the theology of the cross and this radical aesthetics moves toward eschatological hope. This is the third point that Thomsen lifts up in Luther's theology.

Finally, this radical acceptance of sinners based on divine love is connected with the doctrine of creation. Luther offered *"finitum capax infiniti"* in the controversy with Zwingli regarding the real presence of Christ in the Eucharist. Thomsen argues that Luther's formula of the real presence of Christ "in, with, and under" creation led Luther to affirm God's presence in the world. Here, the entire creation is reached by the mercy of God in the light of eschatological hope. Luther's central conviction lies in the agency of God in the world in a non-regular way. Because of the divine affirmation of the creation in an irregular way, Thomsen is also convinced that this worldly commitment to mission for justice and human well-being is essential to join *missio dei*. *Missio dei* is tied with the "divine metacosmic love" in the broken world.

Revelation in the Midst of a Broken World

Thomsen's theology of the cross is a theology of revelation that focuses on the divine metacosmic love. He summarizes his contextual theology of the cross to disclose the divine love in seven claims. First, the cross of Jesus is the consequence of the movement of the reign of God that

---

18. Luther, "Heidelberg Disputation," 57.

Jesus launched: "The cross means dying to private dreams in order to participate in the vision of the kingdom of God."[19] The understanding of the cross is rooted in the historical event of Jesus's life and ministry and his followers. This movement was not aimed at merely individual conversion in a modern evangelical sense. He defines conversion as "conversion to the kingdom of God or the *missio dei*, God's vision of a new creation."[20] Second, Jesus's proclamation of the kingdom of God was also the proclamation of divine solidarity with life, pain, and suffering in the world. Third, he points to the fact that Jesus's ministry of the proclamation of the kingdom of God occurred in the midst of the battle with embodied evil. Thomsen acknowledges, "Sin as embodied evil has incredible power in the world."[21] The cross sheds light on the depth of suffering caused by embodied evil in the world.

Fourth, these directions to see the cross in the historical perspective, such as Jesus's life and ministry, embodied evil, and people's struggles in their lives, are compatible with type C, which González presents in his typology of Christian thought. Type C is none other than the liberative perspective. While Type C does not allow for eliminating historical concern from any theological words, it takes seriously the ability of the incarnation and resurrection to make a historical perspective. Thomsen argues the reason of the cross of Jesus along this line when he says: "Jesus was not sent to die: he came to live and challenge Satan and all his powers. Jesus was crucified in God's struggle for righteousness, truth and the transformation of life."[22]

Fifth, since God took the incarnation to the death on the cross, divine activity is nonviolent against violence. Jesus is the one who is victimized by violence as well as the mass of "crucified people." This is the meaning of scandal that Yacob Tesfai discusses. The "cruciformed *missio dei*" does not hesitate to recognize vulnerability in God. The life, ministry, and death of Jesus transparently showed divine vulnerability. Therefore, unlike the Hellenistic tradition of divine nature, Thomsen af-

19. Ibid., 23.
20. Ibid., 23.
21. Ibid., 25. Gustaf Aulén rediscovered this element in Luther's theology of the cross at the beginning of the twentieth century, which is rooted in the church fathers. However, the difference between Aulén and Thomsen lies in the fact that Thomsen does not overlook the decisive element, that the battleground with Satan is not merely mythical but a reflection of the real world, a real struggle with embodied evil in people's lives.
22. Ibid., 26.

firms that the vulnerability of God does not stop at suffering. Rather, through God's own suffering, God shows the depth of the love for human beings in a miraculous way. The depth of the love "embraces not only victims but also victimizer."[23] In the vulnerable form, the theology of the cross can speak about all in all in reconciliation with the crucified God. Finally, the theology of the cross is a signpost of God's unconditional love and grace. It entails openness to the diversity of a wide variety of human beings.[24]

Thomsen's theology of the cross is primarily a theology of revelation. The content revealed is connected with the form of revelation. The knowledge of God on the cross is not propositional knowledge; it rather entails something that is beyond our form of knowledge (i.e., the indispensable nature of faith). What faith trusts is the heart of the universe that became concrete in Jesus.[25] What is revealed to faith is the breadth and depth of vulnerable and suffering love in the bottom of the world. The divine metacosmic love entails a historical form of Jesus's crucifixion, which is the revelation in the midst of struggling and agony. Therefore, this revelation is not merely logos but the heart of God on the opposite side of what appears on the surface. The heart of God is mirrored in cruciformed creatures. The divine heart is divine activity in history. Divine activity leads our broken world and history to divine consummation of the creation. What Jesus's life, ministry, and death presented is the cruciformed *missio dei*. The invitation to the cruciformed *missio dei* means discipleship inscribed by the cross. Atonement theories must function as witnessing to this heart of God. Otherwise, any discourse falls into a power relationship in the name of God. Ultimately, Thomsen judges any atonement theory from this point when he says, "This understanding of the atonement has nothing to do with the glorification of suffering or divine child abuse. It has nothing to do with the appeasement of a God of wrath. It has everything to do with divine compassion, which is so powerful and deep that love spontaneously embraces all humanity."[26]

Reconstructing a theology of the cross embodied in Jesus's life and ministry, Thomsen presents the other side of a theology of the cross, which many Lutheran theologians, like Forde, overlook.[27] The crucial

23. Ibid., 30.
24. Ibid., 33.
25. Ibid., 38.
26. Ibid., 31.
27. Thomsen elaborates on the critical conversation with Forde's theology of the

point between Thomsen and Forde is the fact that the cause of suffering can be interpreted not only as the alien work of God but also by evil. Whatever one identifies as the cause of suffering, the crucial point that Lutheran scholars clarify is how to lift up the agency of God, whether salvation from the wrath of God or liberation from evil. Enhancing the form of the liberation model, which González calls type C, Thomsen represents the liberative perspective of missiology on the basis of the divine metacosmic love revealed on the cross.

Theology of the Cross in Religious Pluralism

The cruciformed mission of God that Jesus's ministry embodied takes its perspective on religious pluralism in the twenty-first–century global context.[28] While Thomsen evaluates a creative way that pluralism theology advocates, he still insists on his radical inclusivism in order to prioritize the heart of God embodied in history, not to absolutize it as much as to exclude the other religious position.

In his investigation of religious pluralism, especially Knitter's theology of religions, Thomsen finds a decisive deficiency. As a leading thinker in religious pluralism, Knitter has transformed his own theological assumptions through his astonishing dialogue with other religions and other theological positions from Christocentrism through Theocentrism to soteriocentrism.[29] Knitter takes it seriously to be in dialogue with pluralism, and later, with the response from the inclusivist camp, and finally advocates soteriocentrism, which makes it possible to cooperate with other religions for the consummation of the reign of God. While he advocates elevating the liberation perspective, he is very sensitive not to violate the dignity of other religions. However, he weakens the uniqueness of Jesus and the concreteness of the Christian message when he formulates a "multi-normative approach to religious pluralism."[30] Knitter ascribes the uniqueness of Jesus to the announce-

---

cross in the chapter 2 of *Crucified Christ*.

28. Thomsen's latest writing about the theology of religions is *Jesus, the Word, and the Way of the Cross*.

29. Knitter, *Jesus and the Other Names*.

30. Thomsen, *Christ Crucified*, 67. The summarizes of Knitter's position: 1) Jesus is not the full revelation, but universal in having meaning for people; 2) Jesus's revelation is not definitive or unsurpassable but decisive; and 3) Jesus Christ is not constitutive but representational.

ment of the kingdom of God, while the event of revelation and salvation in the name of Jesus becomes surpassable.

Regarding this, Thomsen criticizes Knitter for undercutting the other aspects of Jesus's uniqueness, which are indispensable for Thomsen's cruciformed *missio dei*. Jesus's life and death, which make transparent God's unconditional and passionate love, and his disciples' reception of this compassionate love through Jesus's life and death, evaporate from Knitter's viewpoint. It is not his intention to absolutize the historical dimension of Jesus. Rather, the loss of Jesus's spirituality, the unconditional love concretized in Jesus, and the reception through them is connected with the memory of people who came to the revelation of divine love in the midst of death, violence, desperation, sorrow, weakness, betrayal, and unbelief. This is not a problem of historical inquiry but is a problem of the character of revelation for Christianity. Both Thomsen and Knitter agree that revelation is beyond any particular historical event, whether past or present or whether Christianity or other religions. However, in any time and any place, as long as one who receives revelation is a human being, revelation happens in a particular time and place. Faithfulness to the past event of revelation is simultaneously connected with faithfulness to the present event of revelation among people. From this viewpoint, the reduction of the uniqueness of Jesus into the announcement of the kingdom of God can fall prey to abstraction apart from Knitter's intention. Just as M. M. Thomas proposes, faithfulness to the historical past event of revelation embodied in Jesus does not go hand in hand with imperialism or violence with other religions.[31] Rather, Thomsen proposes that the concrete form and context of revelation embodied in Jesus's life and death and spirituality provide a criterion for Christian self-understanding to open itself to religious dialogue.[32]

Thomsen developed his theology of the cross in a global-mission context. This context is also the place where the symbol of the cross has been under criticism in terms of conflation of imperialism, colonialism, triumphalism, expansionism, and so on. While he is keenly sensitive to these issues, he still develops the cruciformed missiology by using a paradoxical revelation in the cross. Focusing on the metacosmic love of the Abba that Jesus proclaimed, even Good Friday can be a profound moment of God's self-manifestation of love *in, against,* but *for* the world.

31. Thomas, "A Christ-centered Humanist Approach."
32. Thomsen, *Christ Crucified,* 76.

He shows a new frame of mission in the post-Constantinian mission in the midst of massive suffering and injustice. Doing so in a North American context, Thomsen invites people to participate in this divine cruciformed mission with vulnerable love.

EPISTEMOLOGY OF THE CROSS: MARY M. SOLBERG

Thomsen inextricably connects a theology of the cross with the life and ministry of Jesus and presents the heart of God embodied in Jesus's life and death. The cross is a place both to uncover the reality of suffering and to reveal the compassionate pain of God. Only in the paradoxical connection can Jesus's cross be the revelation of God. However, how does one come to the paradoxical revelation of the cross? How does revelation relate a human faculty of knowing? Luther proposed that experience, not speculation, makes it possible to receive the knowledge of God. Reflecting on Luther's existential struggle with the knowledge of God, Solberg proposes her own theology of the cross in a contemporary liberative perspective.

Solberg proposes a way of knowing how to ethically to live with others from her constructive theology of the cross. She considers Luther's theology of the cross as a theology of event, in which his epistemology was broken down and led to "call the thing what it actually is." She expands the event of "epistemological break" to develop theological ethics. She calls it the "epistemology of the cross."[33] The epistemology of the cross is a heuristic device used to practice knowing ethically with others on the basis of the connection between knowing and living. On this point, she thinks that her epistemology of the cross can be in solidarity with secular liberation movements in terms of intellectual praxis by way of promoting our "hermeneutics of suspicion" with regard to epistemology.

The Perspective of Epistemology of the Cross

Her book is a philosophical and theological reflection on epistemology with her experience in El Salvador. She says that her experience in El Salvador was a "transformation of a way of knowing."[34] Through living in El Salvador, she came face to "face with a reality that had never been

---

33. Solberg, *Compelling Knowledge*.
34. Ibid., viii.

real to me before."³⁵ She had known the poverty and suffering of people even before she lived there, but it was just information. Her own flesh prompted her to alter the nature of her knowledge from mere information to acknowledgment. Knowledge being received as acknowledgment compelled her to act in a different way. It influenced her way of life through knowing differently. This brought about the transformation of an ethical attitude toward what she acknowledged. Through this experience, she came to know the fact that there are multiple dimensions in terms of knowing/knowledge. When we talk about knowing or knowledge as acknowledgment, we are compelled to know something in a different way from receiving mere information. That is a kind of experience of conversion in terms of epistemology. There, we come to see what we did not see in the same thing or event. She tried to cut off these dimensions of knowing in order to construct a way of knowing ethically with others. This reflection is devoted not to the poor but to those who live in North America, as she does it in order to truly live with others.

Her project is led by entering a dialogue with double interlocutors: Luther's theology of the cross and secular feminist philosophers. While she embarks on a dialogue with each of them, she is convinced that both can be compatible in that both challenge the dominant epistemology in their own age. Both question a fundamental point of knowing: the question concerning the framework of knowing. Before one knows something, one has already been involved with one's own epistemological frame. What happens when we say, "We know"? Early in the book, she addresses this issue in a conversation with secular feminist epistemologies, which challenge the dominant philosophy of epistemology.

She summarizes the contributions of feminist epistemologies into three points. First, they show the importance of the role of embodied, lived experience. Second, they are suspicious of the central epistemological notion of "objectivity." And third, their aim is to make the knower accountable—that is, to propose a counter-epistemology against a single, abstract epistemology. They also try to restore elements that the dominant epistemology cast away as meaningless in terms of knowing.³⁶ These reflections converge in one idea, which knowledge entails embodiment:

---

35. Ibid., ix.

36. Ibid., 5. According to Solberg, what philosophical epistemology questions is "certainty" in terms of knowing something after René Descartes. In this project, historical or cultural assumptions are cast out of the inquiry.

> Knowledge is situated: shaped, limited, and specified by the locations of knowers, by their particular experiences, by what works for them and what society permits to work for them, by what matters to them and to other knowers with more power, by what they trust and value and whether their objects of trust and value carry any weight in their surroundings. The relationship between what, and how, and for what knowers know, and any or all of these factors, is reciprocal and dialectic.[37]

Therefore, feminist epistemologies challenge an epistemological claim on a single, universal, objective truth in terms of human knowledge. Such a claim ends up with abstracting embodied knowledge in ordinary life. In the same way, it binds one to an illusion that one can live neutrally. But knowledge is contextualized in knowers, and the feminist project aims to expose the co-relational tie between knowing and living. Solberg's attention is drawn to Luther for this reason. For her, Luther is an appropriate interlocutor with feminist philosophers, as she recognizes Luther's way of thinking based on everyday life as significant perspective for its ethical freight.[38]

This point leads her to focus on Luther's theology of the cross, because the theology of the cross as a theology of revelation appeals most to her dialogical approach to feminist epistemologies. For Solberg, as well as Thomsen and Westhelle, Luther's theology of the cross presents his epistemological key. Luther's theology of revelation from the cross encounters the feminist praxis of epistemology. She tries to weave the epistemological challenges that both raise in her epistemology of the cross.

What Is Luther's Theology of the Cross in Her Context?

When Solberg brings Luther into a dialogue with feminist epistemologies, the theology of revelation meets a theological epistemology. First, Solberg argues that there is common ground between Luther and feminist epistemologies. Both emphasize the fragmentedness of knowledge. Knowledge is not separable from existential consciousness. Both also challenge the myth of a single truth that dominant powers propose. Accordingly, both epistemological proposals include protest against power. Then, knowledge of truth and God come through one's own lived experience. For instance, Luther's justification by faith is rooted in his

---

37. Ibid., 9.
38. Ibid., 12–13.

recognition of the agency of God through Jesus Christ. She explains: "It was not man who humbled himself—it was God who humbled him."[39] Knowing the agency of God, not "I," shows the heart of the Reformer in that our knowledge should be overwhelmed by divine self-revelation to us. Our knowing is not equal to divine knowledge. Nobody can systematize the knowledge of God without reservation because it is just a human construction. What we are allowed to do is *passively* to receive something beyond *our* knowledge. This is Luther's confession when he experiences compelling (irresistible) knowledge from God. Therefore, Luther's theology of the cross is primarily a theology of revelation. It is not a theory about revelation in the first place. From the beginning to the end, it is the matter of experience through faith.

Solberg argues that the dynamism between revelation and knowing that appears in Luther's theology of the cross brings about three developments in his lived context. First, Luther's theology of the cross functions as a critique of power. Luther's knowing (discovery) of justification by reason of divine agency led him to an epistemological break. This break changed the way he saw the church, its theology (theology of glory), and the system of grace (indulgence). Here, he finds the rejection of divine agency replaced by human knowledge. With this recognition, he cannot avoid confronting the dominant power. The critique of power is a primary sign of a theology of the cross. Second, she notes the function of announcement. The theology of the cross engages in announcement of divine agency in the event of the cross. At the same time, divine agency has committed to our knowing and living in our own cross situations. It shows "God's disposition toward humankind."[40] Therefore, the theology of the cross announces that "by coming to the world in the human suffering form of Jesus, God is revealed as one who loves and suffers with humanity."[41] Finally, the theology of the cross functions as equipment. The function of equipment means "the way we live."[42] The knowledge of God through Christ was revealed in an unexpected way in the living context of Luther, who was struggling from the double abnegation of his personal suffering and his "success" in practicing monastic life. When he abandoned his own way to accomplish salvation and accepted actual

---

39. Ibid., 66.
40. Ibid., 80.
41. Ibid., 81.
42. Ibid., 84.

divine agency within himself, he knew the way to live with God ethically. Knowledge of God was no longer just information but embodied knowledge in his life. This understanding leads Solberg to contend that "living, not salvation, is what both theologians and theology ought to be concerned about."[43]

In her project, Luther's theology of the cross converges in a theological epistemology. In the case of Luther, the primary concern lies in the knowledge of God. This knowledge is connected with faith. Faith enables us to receive the knowledge of God. The knowledge of God comes from outside a human being. God reveals himself to us. God works for us through Christ. But Solberg rightly sees the other dimension of this self-revelation of God. God reveals us to ourselves and works *within* us. The self-revelation that is received by a human being is not just abstract or objective information outside us. The subjectivity of God cannot be divided into a subject-object dichotomy. That the self-revelation becomes the knowledge of God means that it requests human commitment: "compelling knowledge." However, the agency that brings this knowledge remains God. Solberg's epistemology, through her study of Luther, shows that knowing is accomplished by the Other's working. The Other teaches her the necessity for others to know. To know something about God means to know something that God has already worked for and within us. Luther gained the authentic work of God through his theology of the cross. From the cross, he came to justification by faith. It *compelled* him to live with Christ's life and death in his own life and world.

In sum, Solberg proposes her epistemology of the cross with four components: 1) about power; 2) about experience; 3) about objectivity; and 4) about accountability. When one gets some information, the epistemology of the cross presents an epistemological agenda toward knowing ethically. It allows us to critically rethink information in relation to power. It makes us question whether the knowing process excludes experience: "Lived experience is the locale and the medium of all knowing."[44] Therefore, the epistemology of the cross is willing to open

---

43. Solberg, "Epistemology of the Cross," 140. It is type C in González's typology that Solberg develops Luther's theology of the cross into theological ethics, when she says: "it [theology of the cross] rejects both moralism . . . legalism. . . . It illuminates . . . what Luther called a constant dying and rising with Christ," in *Compelling Knowledge*, 87.

44. Solberg, *Compelling Knowledge*, 112.

its way to other ways of knowing.[45] This leads to rejection of a single-minded objectivism. Solberg does not simply discard the use of objectivity, but she carefully proposes a strategic objectivity, while agreeing with Harding's proposal of "strong objectivity":

> Peculiar strength rests on the participation of many knowers, and among them, begins with the least favored, and a commitment to critical examination of the causes of belief, especially those that have long passed for "objective truths."[46]

What is at stake for Solberg is not a simple equality among knowers but rather to lift up voices that are submerged by the dominant voice. The principle is not egalitarianism but a strategic affirmation of liberation theology: the "preferential option for the poor and the oppressed." This does not mean the ontological privilege of poverty and oppression. Instead, it means that not until we recognize the partiality of our knowledge can we understand this preferential option. The partiality, not the wholeness that objectivity is willing to guarantee, is the signpost of an epistemology of the cross. The emphasis on partiality in a paradoxical way includes not only openness to others but also an acknowledgment of selves concealed even by subjects, as she explains:

> We may discover such places as we look in the mirror at our individual, stitched-together selves. . . . We may also discover places of pain, difficulty, confusion, suffering, in the intersections among these individual and corporate identities, which is where we often come to existential terms with dilemmas that seem to pit us against ourselves and one another.[47]

Therefore, the epistemology of the cross makes it possible to encounter otherness, both in ourselves and others. Knowledge of object evades knowledge of subject and vice versa. The epistemology of the cross attends to the nature of interdependency in terms of epistemology. The primary concern for Luther is the relationality between God and human beings (*coram Deo*). Similarly, the epistemology of the cross creates accountability with others in knowing something or someone (*coram mundo*). The binary distinction between subject and object is evaded

---

45. Ibid., 112–3. It is worth noting that she admits the compatibility with narrative theory, by which feminist theologians make it possible to show embodied truth.

46. Ibid., 121–2. See also Harding, *Whose Science?*

47. Ibid., 120.

by knowing ethically. This brings about the quality of transformation in our activity of knowing: "An epistemology of the cross owes its view of the created world to faith's conviction of the transformative solidarity of God with the world."[48]

The epistemology of the cross is the other side of a theology of the cross as a theology of revelation. Revelation never occurs in a vacuum. It is an event in which Luther came to an "epistemological break" in terms of God, the self, and the world. Solberg contends that Luther's theology of the cross is congruent with a critique of a dominant system of knowledge, which insists on a single authority for truth. It helped him see the falsity of the theology of glory and step outside the vicious cycle of the "technology of grace." The other side of Luther's way toward knowing God in his life and suffering is the theology of the cross. Whenever revelation is spoken, one becomes entwined in an epistemological issue: a question about knowing and knowledge. What conditions make it possible to know something about God? How can one say, "I know him/her or this/that"?

These questions belong to a fundamental issue that Solberg tackles through her conversations with Luther and feminist philosophers of epistemology. Like Luther's theology of the cross, the epistemology of the cross seeks embodied knowledge in human beings' ordinary lives and bodies. It is partial, but it retains embodiment. Because of this partiality, the epistemology of the cross can be open to others' knowledge in the sense of "strong objectivity." Not until our epistemological frames are shaken in encounter with the other are we led to a different picture of reality. The theology of the epistemology strategically rejects a will to get a single-objective "truth" and passionately opens one's own partiality of knowledge to others. Her critical reflection on Luther's theology of the cross is congruent in its critique of power, the strategic acceptance of partiality of knowledge, and openness to other in terms of knowing. In a word, it is the other side of the accountability of knowing with Other/others. The revelation of the cross is nothing other than the knowledge of God revealed "in" us, not in any other place. Luther's theology of the cross helps Solberg start from the foot of the cross in her life and world. However, the cross is more than our referential point to know ethically. It is a historical event. It is not *our* event primarily; it is *his* cross. There is something that cannot be dissolved into *our* knowledge even if it is accountable for others. How does a theology of the cross take into con-

---

48. Ibid., 124–5.

sideration the relation between *ours* and *his*? How can we listen to the voice of the cross? This is the next issue in the following section.

BETWEEN WORLDS: VITOR WESTHELLE

The cross represents the "thorns of history" (Hegel). From the beginning, Christianity has been engaged in interpreting the cross event of Jesus. It is also a history of use and abuse of the cross. A theology seeks a meaning of the cross and at the same time conceals the other dimension of the cross. We come to know the limitations of our knowledge through the cross. Our way of looking into the cross relates to our way of viewing our world. In this context, Westhelle clarifies a basic condition of the cross and the world; it is conditioned by representation. A theology of the cross discloses one's own world and at the same time, conceals. While maintaining our limitations, he tries to touch on divine drama in the midst of the cross in the analogy of Shabbat in Jewish-Christian tradition. It is not a new discourse or a new theological content. Rather, his theology of the cross is a kind of letter that invites readers to seek cracks in our world through the divine work of "faith desiring":

> This story of scandal and promise is like the Shabbat, the day God takes a break, does nothing, when we are given the holy right to pray and play. But this Shabbat is also the day we mourn the death of God, God in all of creation that God has assumed in order to redeem.... which swings between two realities that God died and God lives.[49]

The swinging rhythm between God died and God lives cuts into our intellectual swinging rhythm between disclosing and concealing.

Theology of Anfechtungen/Tentatio

Westhelle finds subversive elements in Luther's way of doing theology. He links them to something that rejects systematization. Luther's theological method is far from the abstract, thematic method that was dominant in Luther's age. Rather, doing theology is inseparable from the subject's way of living. Regarding Luther's struggle over the matter of indulgence, Solberg points out that Luther suffered from the feeling of abnegation not only in an individual and spiritual sense, but also in a socio-political sense. What Luther confronted was surely his abnegation

---

49. Westhelle, *Scandalous God*, x–xi.

because of his awareness of sinfulness and divine wrath, but he also went further. Westhelle also pushes this point, specifying a particular context that a theology of the cross challenges.

As Kurt Hendel and other scholars have already argued, Luther's theology is indistinguishable from his experience of suffering.[50] In the tradition of scholasticism traced to Aristotle, human experience should be disregarded in theological inquiry because any experience is entangled with contingency and does not deserve being related to the search for truth.[51] The Hellenistic binalism was active in Luther's age and even today. Considering the history of theological methods, Luther's reflection on his own suffering is revolutionary in that he cuts through the binalism. He drastically deconstructed the medieval theological method and reconstructed his own way by doing theology from his own suffering context. This made Luther replace *contemplatio* with *tentatio* in the medieval tripartite rules for theology from *lectio, oratio, and contemplatio* into *oratio, meditation,* and *tentatio*. The translation of *tentatio* is *Anfechtungen* in German, meaning "trial, test, and being under attack." Luther's theology of the cross is grounded in the theology of tentatio. It is a way of doing theology from the foot of the cross/his own tentatio. A theology of the cross is neither a formula of theology nor one section of Christian doctrine. Rather, it exposes the crack in any discourse of God, human beings, and the world. He calls it an "epistemological gesture." Therefore, Luther preferred the expression a theologi-*an* of the cross to a theo-*logy* of the cross. A theology of the cross is a disposition to live from the foot of the cross.

Luther's Tentatio/Anfechtung

Luther's fundamental pre-Reformation question was, "How can I meet the merciful God?" Just as well known, this question led him to justification by faith with Christ alone. It was not an easy path that led Luther to come to justification by faith. The more he practiced monastery piety, the more he deepened his agony and anxiousness in terms of divine wrath and justice. He certainly experienced his spiritual agony. However, the question of justice, which prompted his religious practice, ironically pulled him down to suffering deeper than his psychological, individual,

---

50. Hendel, "Theology of the Cross," 223–31.
51. Bayer, *Theology the Lutheran Way,* 28–32.

or spiritual suffering. Regarding the suffering of Luther, Solberg provides a clue when she attempts to seek Luther's Anfechtungen in relation to his struggle with power. Solberg sees in Luther's resistance against a theology of glory something more than a theological argument for individual soul-salvation because the theology of glory was not merely a coherent system of theology but functioned to be compatible with and support a dominant system: politics, economics, and law. She calls this order of power in which a theology of glory joined "technology of grace":

> The medieval church provided a seemingly never-ending stream of "products," in addition to confession, the purchase or practice of which might demonstrate the desire of a believer to do that "extra little something" in him or her, made realizable by a kind of ecclesial "technology" of grace.[52]

We can see Luther's spiritual agony rooted in his awareness of sinfulness within himself from one point of view. But from the other point of view, we can also see that his perception of sin and his religious practice for emancipation are entangled within the framework of the "technology of grace." When he encountered justification by faith in Jesus Christ, not by human accomplishment, he was simultaneously emancipated both from his feeling of abnegation and from the frame by which people lived and died. That is precisely the point Westhelle makes in terms of Luther's theology of the cross. It does not exclude Luther's spiritual and individual agony when he lost sight of God's grace, and it also does not reject the fact that Luther had externally struggled with the ecclesial and political power of his day.[53] There is something more complicated that cannot be reduced either into the inner or the external—a struggle with the system of knowledge that is rooted in all human life to live within the society. Many Luther scholars turn Luther's struggle into universally human sinfulness against God. However, Westhelle jumps into an intra-contextual reading between liberation theology and Luther and presents liberative practice against a dominant system of knowledge in Luther's struggle.[54] The justification by faith that Luther brought into the foreground of the Reformation can be understood in light of the contextual battle about the understanding of God's justice in his age.

52. Solberg, *Compelling Knowledge*, 62–63.

53. The latest work about Luther's theology of the cross in light of social theory is Ruge-Johnes, *Cross in Tensions*.

54. Thomsen, review of *Scandalous God*, 465–6.

Westhelle argues that Anselm's satisfaction theory paved the ground for the doctrine of salvation in that age. The principle that established the satisfaction theory officially came from the prevailing understanding of justice not only theologically but also juristically. That is the principle of the *suum cuique* (*to each what to each is due*), which was pervasive in the "earthly economies of regimes."[55] A generation later, Abelard contradicted Anselm's idea, when he was convinced that the principle could not solve the case, "If for a relatively minor sin of failing to give due to honor to God such sacrifice and punishment was required, who will now make the payment for humanity's having killed the very Son of God?"[56] Then, he tried to resolve the contradiction by inserting the principle of love. But Luther asked a more profound question than Abelard's: "Is God's justice ruled by the *suum cuique* principle?"[57] Finally, Luther expresses his discovery in the lectures on Isaiah 53: "Behold the new definition of justice: justice is the knowledge of Christ."[58] Westhelle continues to explain the decisiveness of this definition: "The genitive in cognicio Christi is double: it is to know about Christ (objective genitive) and also to have the knowledge Christ had (subjective genitive)."[59]

Luther also introduced a soteriological term to explain salvation: "wonderful exchange." The teaching of wonderful exchange in relation with the double knowledge of Christ shows not only the one side of happy exchange that Christ takes our place but also the other side of wonderful exchange that we are allowed to take the place of Christ (subjective genitive). Here, the concept of the second sense brought about a "scandalous subversion of the venerable maxim": "to us what is not due to us, as well to others what is not due to them."[60] What Luther brought through his new definition of justice goes beyond and shakes down the juridical concept of justice. Instead, justice comes from the knowledge of Christ (*for* and *in* us). Divine justice is totally a gift of divine grace: "the justice of Christ transgresses their wisdom and legislations."[61]

55. Westhelle, *Scandalous God*, 38, 42.
56. Ibid., 39.
57. Ibid., 39.
58. Ibid., 39, quoting from Luther, "Lectures on Isaiah," 229.
59. Ibid., 40.
60. Ibid., 39.
61. Ibid., 42.

The double knowledge of Christ (for and in us) is transgressive over the world's régimes. The knowledge of Christ breaks into the crack between language and event itself. Luther's sensitivity to abnegation and the knowledge of Christ met the crack between the discourses of sin, suffering, the cross, and Christ, all of which were put into a system. His personal agony rising from abnegation took root not merely in his personal psychological problem but in a much deeper human condition. Human knowledge kills human beings. The cross triggered the epistemological break between what the system of knowledge (law) knows and what a theologian of the cross knows. Luther, learning from Paul, brought his fundamental question, how to meet the God of grace, to the foot of the cross: "What can I know of God in the face of the cross or according to the cross (*kata stauron*)? The knowledge of Christ enables a theologian of the cross to call "the thing what it actually is."[62] It is an invitation to step out of the "régimes of truth" in solidarity with suffering people.

Creatively connecting a theology of the cross with a postmodern critique of the régime of truth, Westhelle proposes a new key for a theology of the cross apart from conventional keys. That is the *epistemic* key. Traditionally, a theology of the cross has been practiced in response to two sorts of questions. Each of them is exemplified by Anselm and Abelard. Westhelle asks the question that Anselm raised and stimulates the *apoteletic* key (accomplishment) and that of Abelard's "moral key."[63] The *apoteletic* key raises the question of "what the cross is in and of itself."[64] On the other hand, the moral key raises another question, "What does the cross move me to do?" Each question provides a framework to respond to human questions. Both are important to reflect on the traditional trajectory about the cross. However, Westhelle brings a third key, which does not emerge from these keys. He calls it the *epistemic* key. The question that the epistemic key brings appears by distinguishing a theology of the cross from a theology *about* the cross. This key is a kind of "epistemological gesture," which Westhelle considers as an indispensable element of a theology of the cross: It "places the question of the relationship between cross and suffering on another key."[65] "Why did Jesus die? Why do people suffer? What is the relationship between these two

---

62. Luther, "Heidelberg Disputation," 53.
63. Westhelle, *Scandalous God*, 42.
64. Ibid., 76.
65. Ibid., 84.

questions?"⁶⁶ The *epistemic* key does not exclude the other keys. Rather, Westhelle attempts to insert this key into any question about the cross, because the key itself implies an answer.

Why Did Jesus Die?

Westhelle simply answers that the reason Jesus died is because of his naming suffering as it is: "Jesus died on the cross because he named the law that kills and practiced the healing that restores. He did it by stepping precisely into the margin of the law . . . by transgressing it."⁶⁷ The suffering of Jesus is derived from his "naming ministry." When Westhelle makes such an assertion, he actually recognizes the limits of the world and the limits of the discourse. Discourse is different from the reality to which the discourse points. It is not good or evil. It is the condition of *our* world. The problem is, when we inhabit one certain world framed by discourse/knowledge, we are not aware of this limitation. One system of knowledge excludes the other. The cross event itself presents the problem of frame.

Jesus practiced transgressing the frame of *his* world in which he and his people lived and died. He exposed the "law that kills." The epistemic key that Jesus had already practiced is a "strategic invitation in which one is led to the margin of the text, to the frame of the picture." That is the power of fragmentation rooted in the "knowledge of Christ." Jesus practiced the "knowledge of Christ" in the sense of "subjective genitive" of a double knowledge of Christ. The abyss of the cross sheds light on the abyss of our knowledge. However, only from the abyss can the knowledge of Christ appear in us: "The possibility of divine justice in the midst of this world manifest themselves precisely where these economies and regimes break down or are transgressed."⁶⁸ The *epistemic* key distinguishes and at the same time connects Jesus's cross with the crosses of innocent people. His cross is the consequence of his ministry in a way that boldly asked why they suffer. Jesus's "naming ministry" is resonant with Foucault's concept of *"parrhesis"* (to speak the truth boldly) and Gandhi's *"satyagraha"* (truth-force) in that they all place themselves at the margin of the system and speak truth at the cost of their lives. All of

66. Ibid., 84.
67. Ibid., 85.
68. Ibid., 42.

them transgress the frameworks of knowledge that killed their people. This is the insurrection of the *word of the cross* (the *logos tou staurou*) in the context of people's suffering. Westhelle also proposes a new method of doing a theology by following the spirit of the Reformation. It alludes to a theological paradigm shift.

The Paradigm Shift of Faith/Theology

Westhelle presents the reformulation of his theological methodology from faith understanding (*fides quaerens intellectum*) to faith desiring. Anselm's phrase, *fides quaerens intellectum*, which is a popular definition of theology in the Western tradition, uses the verb *quaero* as a transitive verb. However, Westhelle reforms this formula into its intransitive understanding—that is, "faith seeking" or "theology is faith desiring." Here, faith is not an object of theology. Nobody can possess, analyze, or objectify it. Westhelle's theology of the cross strikes at this point. The theology of the cross does not deal with any object that faith seeks. Rather, faith desiring retains "the intransitive desiring in solitude (which is desiring nothing but *faith itself*)," while the *apoteletic* key responds to "an external object (promise and hope)" and the moral key to a "pure relationality as its object (which is love)."[69]

First, since faith is the subject, it means that I/we are not the subject in a usual way. This represents his acceptance of intransitive activity, which cannot be reduced to an independent human subject. Westhelle does not necessarily exclude the definition of faith in the sense of objective or subjective atonement. However, the third element of *faith desiring* functions to shed light on the other elements. Faith desiring remains the subject as it is. Epistemologically speaking, what we can do is nothing independently. We cannot point to it like "here it is, there it is." Faith is neither object nor human notion, but "a divine work in us which changes us and makes us altogether different."[70] This designates the core of Luther's justification by faith. That core is faith alone, but this is not the attribute of pious humans or even a trustful attitude in that place. What we can do is to live a "receptive life (*vita passive*)."[71] Faith desiring is divine action actualizing in the moment of absence.

69. Ibid., 126.

70. Luther, "Preface to the Acts," 370–1.

71. Bayer, *Theology the Lutheran Way*, 23. Bayer finds Luther's revolutionary definition of faith. Faith is the passive life only for God's action. This is neither knowledge nor action.

The cross of Jesus shows a double manifestation of the world in God (the world's rejection of God) and God in the world (God's presence in the world). On the one hand, the justice of Christ comes to the end of death in the cross of Jesus. The power of the world rejected and killed him. This is the condition of the world that kills human beings. On the other hand, faith desiring is present in the moment of absence. The swing between "God died and God lives" turns into "hope against hope" in the moment of absence that the women who witnessed the resurrection of the crucified Jesus in the gospel embodied. The moment of absence is the moment of faith desiring, but it does not mean to *overcome* absence. Rather, it is the *affirmation* of absence. The affirmation of the resurrection is that of the crucified Jesus, who spoke of the knowledge of Christ for them. Faith in Jesus Christ is embodied in those women who practiced "a labor of love and mourning." Westhelle calls it a "practice of resurrection." This is the other side of a theology of the cross.

Faith desiring is unconditional, but the cross is a particular space where faith desiring works. At least, Christianity is rooted in the particular historicity of scars and the particular scars of history. These scars came from a "theology from the cross," which he identifies with the embodied witness in the women:

> The Word that creates, the Word that communicates entails the premonition of a third that does not come, that the poet does not want, but it is here . . . the moment of remembrance, silence, absence, and sacrifice, which we want not—yet reveals the longings of our hearts, minds, and souls where faith alone sustains us against all hope, against all love, that is, against all the flaws in our attempts of creating a better world, against all our lapses in bringing about understanding, discernment, and justice . . . The "third" here is not even a word; it is a sigh, a breath that remains ineffable. Yet this sigh, this breath is also *ruah*, the very spirit of life that then does not compose a discourse, does not utter words.[72]

Only in this sense is the cross *at-one-moment*. It cannot be repeatable. It is not the ground of faith for a theologian of the cross. Rather, the *at-one-moment*, by reason of this *at-one-moment*, sheds light on other *at-one-moments* of absence through the unconditional divine gift of faith desiring. Our lives and deaths swing between the moment of

72. Ibid., 141.

absence and the moment of faith desiring. A theology of the cross is a way of life in which there is nothing without the "third" of faith: intransitive divine presence within *him/her*. That is the reason why Westhelle ponders Shabbat as a precious moment of *theoria*, in which the *theoria* is different from its Aristotelian distinction. It is *theoria* or *contemplation* in a way that makes it possible for us to see divine activity in the moment of absence, the moment that we come to the end of our own *praxis* and *poiesis*, and even *theoria*.

CONCLUSION

Mark Thomsen sees Luther's limitations in terms of his political attitudes because of his individual and spiritual concern. Nevertheless, he does not overlook the sharp insight of Luther to examine the double reality of the world and God in the light of the cross. Solberg critically dialogues with Luther's theology of the cross in order to undergird her own epistemological challenge to current dominant systems of knowledge in connection with power. She sees Luther as the one who existentially struggles with the conflation between power and dominant knowledge. When Luther started seeking the knowledge of God from the foot of the cross, he was convinced that the knowledge of the cross means our knowledge of the world and selves here and now. Therefore, a theology of the cross challenges us to know God without any ethical responsibility for Other/others. Finally, Westhelle suggests that there is a great deal of space for students of Luther to specify his context, to examine Luther as a contextual theologian. For example, he proposes that Luther's understanding of justification by faith is not a reformulation of justice but the new formation of justice against juridical, political, and economic injustice in the world. That is, he connects Luther's knowledge of Christ from the cross with the socio-political knowledge that comes from suffering. What is common between Thomsen, Solberg, and Westhelle is that all attempt to develop a contextual theology of the cross from a liberative perspective.

With this perspective of liberation, they also keep a dialogue with their theological tradition: Luther's theology of the cross. Their way of reading Luther is not to canonize Luther's text but to undertake a dialogue with the great heritage of Luther in order to rethink the tradition in their own theological perspectives. Although they evaluate Luther differently, they agree that they start with Luther's theology of the cross to seek knowledge of God, human beings, and the world. Luther's theology of the cross helps them to think about God in the midst of the cruelty, limitations, demonization, and idolization of the world. However, it is more important than the commonality of the contents to see the commonality of their disposition of doing theology. In other words, the three theologians find the intersection between Luther and their liberative perspective in a theological method rather than mere theological content. They read Luther in light of orthopraxis. Luther's theology of the cross in light of orthopraxis is relevant to Segundo's comment on methodology: "The one and only thing that can maintain the liberative character of any theology is not its content but its methodology."[73] That is an indispensable point that makes it possible to enact an intercontextual dialogue.

Unlike the general assumption of liberation theology, in which this theology is assumed to be a practical theology for social injustice in the binalism between practice and theory, liberation theology presents a fundamental challenge for intellectual disposition. Theology becomes a way of "articulating one's faith that comes out of one's Christian commitments to a particular way of acting and sets the agenda for an even more thoughtful and committed plan of action in the future."[74] In this regard, John Sobrino clarifies the transformative method of theology from orthodoxy to orthopraxis: "theology finds its fulfillment not in mere 'right thinking' (*ortho-doxy*), but in 'right acting' (*ortho-praxy*)."[75] Specifying Luther's theology of the cross with the aspects of orthopraxis, they take Luther's orthopraxis as a theological method into account.

Luther's theology of the cross involves orthopraxis in its theological methods, by which these theologians reject a metaphysical method to seek knowledge of God, human beings, and the world. Rather, when knowledge is connected with the cross, the knowledge of God is interconnected with the knowledge of human beings or the world. They reject the Aristotelian conviction that truth is not influenced by "experience" and "history." In the case of the Aristotelian-scholastic tradition, this character of knowledge is connected with divine impassibility, omnipotence, and omnipresence. However, what Luther rejects by his theology of the cross is the "pure rational theology" that cannot link our experience and history in terms of God's revelation. In this regard, Luther says, "theol-

---

73. Segundo, *Liberation of Theology*, 39.
74. Bevans, *Models of Contextual Theology*, 72.
75. Ibid., 72.

ogy is experiential wisdom."[76] The revelation of God is nothing out of the world. In other words, revelation is an event that happens in the human experiential world, and it then brings the embodiment of knowledge to our perception of God. Human reason cannot perceive the embodiment of knowledge because reason cannot trust anything contingent on this world in seeking truth and God. Therefore Luther finds the limitation of human reason in theology, because knowledge about God is not a timeless, eternal, and unchangeable object outside our experience and history. Luther's theology of "wisdom" is "a path that unites theory and practice and grounds both in the sense of a receptive life."[77] Wisdom, not science, encourages us to sense revelation in our life and experience and participate in the divine intervention in our life and experience.

Here is a methodological contact point with other contextual theologies. Luther's theology of the cross as orthopraxis seeks wisdom. It is neither *theoria* nor *praxis*. It does not merely allow us to approach the suffering God, but it compels us to start with the knowledge of God from the cross, when we reflect on Luther's words, "Christian theology does not begin with the highest good, as all other religions do, but with the lowest depths, with the womb of Mary and Jesus' death on the cross."[78] Luther's theology of the cross is firmly grounded on his own experience represented by these words: "The cross alone is our theology [*CRUX sola est nostra Theologia*]."[79] This is the reason why the three theologians of the cross read Luther in the light of orthopraxis.

The way of their doing theology, orthopraxis, offers good examples to concretize the three perspectives I presented in the introduction: contextual theology, negotiating with tradition (through Luther's tradition), and intercontextuality (dialogue with other contexts). Although their particular location is in North America, their perspectives are opened to other contextual issues, such as global mission theology, religious pluralism, Latin American liberation theology, feminist theology/philosophy, postmodern philosophy, and postcolonial critiques. As Robert Schreiter understands the interconnection of contextual theologies as a "global flow," these three theologians' perspectives can flow through

---

76. Bayer, *Theology the Lutheran Way*, 29.
77. Ibid., 28.
78. Ibid., 27.
79. Luther, "Operationes in Psalmos," 176.

global theological movements.[80] The point that strikes me is that their contextual method for theologizing is necessarily interconnected with other contextual theologies in a nonsystematic way, showing an alternative to a universal theology that attempts to cover the earth by a single principle. I would like to use a term "ubiquity," rather than "universal" in the global theological flow. Their intercontextual perspectives can be ecumenically and mutually connected with other contextual theologies, while being rooted in their own contexts. The ubiquity of a theology of the cross is grounded on its ability of communication beyond boundaries in a way that makes each contextual theology enter conversation with others on the basis of its own orthopraxis. That is what I mean by "intercontextual reading."

---

80. Schreiter, *New Catholicity,* 15–21. Flow is originally a term of sociology and anthropology. Schreiter explains that the global theological flow, which is represented by liberation, feminism, ecology, and human rights, is a kind of circulating movement with anti-systematic meaning.

2

God in Context

THIS PROJECT WAS ORIGINALLY placed in the context of my concern for the future of Christianity in Japan. Many familiar with the situation of Christianity in Japan share a common question: why does Christianity remain undeveloped? The question has various implications, depending on who asks the question. Some ask it out of an evangelistic concern and others from a socio-political perspective that considers the importance of regional phenomena. Still others ask it when comparing the growth of Christian communities in other regions, or to lament the impact of secularism in the context of Japan. To begin with this particular perspective—that is, being Japanese, Lutheran, and Christian—does not negatively narrow my approach to this project. Rather, I will put these particular aspects into a broader context by engaging them in conversation with global partners. In the current global/theological context, it is almost impossible to limit oneself to any single context. Japan is necessarily connected to neighboring countries and to the global community at the same time. Lutheran confessional conversations occur in an ecumenical context and in dialogue with other religions and secular movements. Diverse theological trends, which flow on a global scale, such as postmodern/colonial discourse, liberation and feminist perspectives, and a theology of religions, produce a contextual and constructive theological argument for a Japanese cultural perspective.

Contextual theology as a theological awareness has existed at least since the 1970s. Just as Bevans argues, it does not mean that contextual theology started at that time. Rather, it claims that any theology is contextual. I surveyed theologies of the cross in the North American context through the lens of contextual theology in the previous chapter. They all develop a theology of the cross from the perspective of orthopraxis. However, moving forward to the Asian context, a theology of the cross meets different kinds of interlocutors religiously, culturally, and intellectually. I will explore Kitamori as the initiator who develops Luther's theology of the cross in the Japanese context. The study of his theology will provide the contextual case for a theology of the cross in a particular context. In the following sections, I will first try to locate the theology of the pain of God in the Japanese religious-cultural context. Then, I will shift my eyes to other Asian theologies of the cross to put Kitamori's context into the larger Asian context. I expect this intercontextual reading of the theology of the pain of God to clarify the contextual issues about a theology of the cross in an Asian context.

OVERVIEW OF THEOLOGY OF THE PAIN OF GOD

Japanese theologian Kazoh Kitamori published *Theology of the Pain of God* in Japan in 1946 just after World War II.[1] Born in 1916 in Kyushu, a southern Japanese island, Kitamori became baptized in the Japanese Lutheran church in high school. He went to Japanese Lutheran seminary and graduated from Kyoto Imperial University, where he enrolled in the classes of Kyoto School's philosophers such as Nishida Kitaro, Tanabe Hajime, and so on. However, he completed his sketch of *Theology of the Pain of God* before encountering the Kyoto School. Kitamori held the position of professor at Tokyo Union Theological Seminary for nearly forty years until he retired. He published more than forty books, and his writings continue to be republished.

The main thesis of his theology is that the heart of the gospel is the pain of God. He acquires the insight of the pain of God from Jeremiah 31:20: "Therefore my heart is broken" (*Darum bricht mir mein Herts*). Following Luther's theology of the cross, he attempts to present the Christian God from the cross. Like Luther, Kitamori's theology is preoccupied with soteriology: salvation by God's love rooted in pain. He explains this notion of love rooted in pain by using the three orders of love. The first order of love is the immediate, smooth, and flowing love to a human being. This first love becomes pain because of human sin, disobedience against God. However, God is determined to embrace fallen humans by reason of God's deepest essence of love. It is not immediate love but the love mediated by the pain of God. The love rooted in the

---

1. Kitamori, *Theology of the Pain*. This writing was first published in Japanese 1946, and has been translated into English, German, Spanish, Italian, and Korean.

pain of God accompanies the forgiveness of sin. The cross is the locus to reveal the "process of his agonies," by which God embraces those who cannot be embraced, forgives those who cannot be forgiven, and loves those who cannot be loved.[2] In order to distinguish between the first order and the third order, Kitamori even criticizes Luther in that he recognizes the "wrath of God" as the "means of revealing God's love." He considers the wrath of God as the *real* reaction of God to *real* sin.[3]

As Kitamori takes his place in the line of Luther's theology, his theology tries to challenge divine impassibility. He understands that it was Luther in particular who put forward the suffering God in his Christology, *communicatio idiomatum* (the communication of attributes). Following Luther's steps, he expands the pain of God into the *essence* of God. He recognizes the contribution of Hellenistic Christianity that clarified the nature of God in terms of *homoousios*, but this contribution also prevents us from perceiving the *heart* of God. Using the term "heart," he attempts to explain the dialectic relationship between an all-embracing God and sinners. As Luther's existential struggle enables him to perceive the agony of God, "God is fighting with God," Kitamori tries to "re-root the gospel of Christ for the Japanese mind."[4] He asserts *itami* (pain) as the key word to search for the heart of God. He believes that the term itami enables Japanese people to access the essence of God in an aesthetic way because what the Japanese associate with the term itami is the connotation of *tsurasa* (bitter feeling), which is well expressed in Japanese tragedy (*kabuki* drama), rather than physical pain. He explains tsurasa like this:

> Tsurasa, the basic principle in Japanese tragedy, is realized when one suffers and dies, or makes his beloved son suffer and die, for the sake of loving and making others live. Even though he tries hard to conceal and endure his agony, his cries filtering through his efforts are heard.[5]

2. Ibid., 22. The phrase, the "process of his agonies" originally derives from Uemura Masahisa (1858–1925). Uemura is the founding theologian in the Japanese Protestant church. He is the one who most influenced Kitamori's theology.

3. It is outstanding among Asian contextual theologians of the cross that he concentrates on the reality of sin. When he says "this age of pain," some feel sure that Kitamori is reflecting on his dark age of the war. In any case, this emphasis on the reality of sin and wrath is also found in Koyama's critical attitude, for Asians, the Japanese in particular, tend to lack an understanding of sin against God.

4. Koyama, *Water Buffalo Theology*, 86.

5. Kitamori, *Theology of the Pain*, 135.

Thus, as itami reminds the Japanese of the aesthetic perception of a tragic event, tsurasa provides a unique way of perceiving the heart of God on the cross. By introducing the itami and the tsurasa, he sets up the aesthetic perception of the cross rather than the rational or juridical understanding.[6] His theology of the cross presupposes a theology of reconciliation on the basis of the satisfaction theory. However, his emphasis is not the idea of punishment or compensation for the dishonor for God but the disclosure of divine acceptance of sinners with his broken heart. This God is an all-embracing God. However, unlike liberalism, which identifies all-embracing love with the first order of love, immediate love, Kitamori's all-embracing God is in love rooted in the pain (the third order of love). The cross is the event that reveals a divine heart, through which the Father lets the Son die by reason of embracing sinners. He presents the embracing of God mediated by the negation of negation: the pain of God.

Kitamori's primary concern is the view of God in the Japanese context. However, surprisingly, in comparison with the responses from abroad both in the West and in East Asia, his theological contribution has not been evaluated highly in this original context.[7] He was never a mainstream theologian in his native Japan.[8] Yagi Seiichi proposes three reasons why Kitamori was not accepted by Japanese theologians. The first is that his severe criticism of Karl Barth conflicted with mainline Protestant theologians who were influenced by Barth's radical dialectics. Second, in spite of his denial, his theology is suspected on patropassionism. Finally, postwar Japanese people were skeptical about their cultural heritage, while Kitamori enthusiastically and critically engaged in dialogue with it.[9] In addition to these external reasons, Yagi also argues that

---

6. Otto, "Japanese Religion in Theology of the Pain," 38–48. Otto criticizes the point that Kitamori's tendency to introduce the aesthetic way takes away from the Bible. I will argue this later.

7. For reactions to a theology of the pain of God from the Western theologians, see Michalson, "Theology of the Pain." Since Michalson introduced the theology of the pain of God into the Western theological circle fourteen years after the publication, Kitamori received many comments from the West. The main Western theologians who refer to Kitamori directly are: Heinrich Otto (1966), Jurgen Moltmann (1972), Dorothe Sölle (1973), Hans Küng (1978), Alister McGrathe (1994), and Douglas John Hall (2003). Regarding the reaction from theologians in Asia, I will discuss this in later sections.

8. Morimoto, foreword of *Theology of the Pain*. See also Miyamoto, *Kami no itami*. This is the first full publication about a theology of the pain of God originally written in Japanese.

9. Yagi, "Third Generation," 88.

Kitamori "should have presented the history of the conception of the pain of God more fully in order to show that it was not heterodox."[10] Kuramatsu Isao, a Japanese Luther scholar, makes the same point from a different perspective:

> I think that the situation (undeveloped discussion about the theology of pain of God in Japan) lies in the fact that it is still difficult to find a criterion and measure to evaluate his theology theologically.[11]

What does Kuramatsu mean by "theologically"? Probably, as an expert of Luther's theology, he may consider that Luther's theological method is not well understood in Japan. This is reasonable, but I will consider the issue from the opposite side; in what context has the theology of the pain of God been placed by Kitamori and been read by others? Some easily imagine from his confrontational style of writing that his theology is too "apologetic."[12] However, as long as I see him in line with Luther's theology of the cross, it is not enough to label it so. It is not a simple apologetic work.[13] Rather, when he has already declared that the theology of the pain of God must continue to stand "outside the gate," he understands how a theology of the cross functions in Christian tradition.[14] His "apologetic" focuses on the view of God in the non-theistic tradition of Japan by firmly standing on the "thin" tradition of Christianity. This is not a metaphysical concern. Rather, it is an apologetic concern in a particular cultural context, which is to disclose the heart of God, not the essence of God, in a strict sense. The heart of God is circumscribed by the principle of "all embracing." In the next sections, I will survey the contextual studies of his "apologetics."

---

10. Ibid., 88.

11. Isao, "Historical Significance of *Theology of the Pain,*" 302–3. Yagi and Kuramatsu, who have been familiar with German theology, seem to allude to the fact that Lutheran tradition is extremely thin in Japan.

12. Takizawa, "On *Theology of the Pain,*" 124. This article is the lecture notes about a theology of the pain of God in Müchen in 1975. There, he points "nein" to Kitamori's theology with his teacher, Karl Barth: "This Japanese Christian is busy in apologetics, the apologetics by the one who studies much about Western theology, but does not deepen it at all, but just forgets the eternally 'primordial fact of IMMANUEL=Christ', or never be awaken to the truth." See also Barth's criticism of Kitamori, preface to *Fukuinshugi shingaku nyumon,* by Barth, 204.

13. On the other hand, it is another reason for some liberal theologians to accuse him of being politically conservative that he showed later in a political conflict in 1960s and 1970s. See Kasahara, "Confession of War Responsibility," 208.

14. Kitamori, *Theology of the Pain,* 150.

GOD IN CONTEXT

"Theology is ultimately concerned with the concept of God. A theology failing to contribute anything decisive to the view of God should not make any final pronouncements."[15] Here Kitamori attempts to open the view of God from the cross. But in what context does he mention it? What is his perspective of "pain"? I will try to clarify these questions.

Translation of God: Xavier

Christian missionaries had difficulty in communicating about their Christian God in Japan from the beginning. Since Francis Xavier started the Jesuit mission to Japan, what Christianity confronts has been a religious-cultural confrontation rather than socio-political. Although the term of inculturation came into theology in the 1970s, Schreiter considers Xavier's way of mission as an excellent example for a current inculturation model.[16] Nevertheless, it is not easy even for him to communicate the term "God." He intended to find a term to communicate Creator to the Japanese, who did not have a systematic way to describe God except in Buddhist terminology. First of all, he used the term *Dainichi*, which is the body of Buddha in the *Shingon* sect of Buddhism, by following his translator. Xavier thought that Dainichi, which was believed to be the origin of all beings, was equivalent to the Creator.[17] He soon came to realize that Dainichi is a kind of energy that cannot have any substance. Then, he changed the name of God to *Deus*, the Latin pronunciation of God. When his colleagues went to the street to proclaim Deus, they encountered difficulty. Deus sounded like "*dai uso*" (big lie) to Japanese ears. They also used *Tenshu* (the lord of heaven) as an alternative. The problem of translation remained when the Protestant missionaries came to Japan at the end of the nineteenth century.[18]

---

15. Ibid., 46.

16. Schreiter, "The Legacy of St. Francis Xavier," 17–31.

17. Suzuki, "Translation of God: Part One," 34. Dainichi Buddha is a kind of original energy that gives birth to all buddhas and bodhsattvas.

18. Ibid., 139–44. Between the first period of mission in Japan in the sixteenth and seventeenth centuries and the second period since the nineteenth century, there was a great deal of debate about the translation of God in China among missionaries. According to Suzuki, such a discussion did not happen in Japan in the process of translation of the name of God in nineteenth-century Japan. See also Chung, "Mission and Inculturation," 303–27.

In 1885, there were sixteen ways of reading the name of God, which were constituted by six combinations of Chinese characters.[19] However, when the New Testament translation was finished in which the translation for God became *Kami* (the same Chinese letter as *Shen* in China), this translation became widely used. This history means that Japanese Christianity has encountered a perennial challenge to distinguish the Christian Kami from the native other kami.[20] I would like to suggest two perspectives from which I will think about the naming of God in the Japanese context at the present. The first one concerns the perspective to stabilize Christian identity and the second one to keep local religious-cultural identity.

The first perspective is found in the first generation of Protestant Japanese theologians, like Uemura Masahisa and Uchimura Kanzo. They are wary of being syncretistic toward their local deity, while they are more well-known for being wary of theological colonialism by Western mission theology.[21] They sought a way to clarify the God witnessed in the Bible by avoiding these two deviations. For example, Uemura compares his faith situation with Paul's in Athena:

> The Athenians worshiped each demon and spirit, and they prayed to numerous idols. Among the idols was one called "The unknown god." When Paul the Apostle saw this, he warmly proclaimed, "You worship without knowing. I tell you, this is the True God." Consider, the people of the world have forgotten God's way, they are lost on the mountain path and don't know how to seek our father who is in heaven.[22]

Suzuki argues that the "true God" was the name for God in Japanese that emerged from these theologians as a consequence of the translation of "God" as Kami. He continues to explain that the distinction between the "true God" and the other kami for theologizing was necessary in order for them to confront the Japanese religious-political combination of imperial *Shinto* Japan:

19. Suzuki, "Translation of God: Part Two," 146.

20. Ibid., 147.

21. Accordingly, the situation of the first generation of Protestant theologians is different from that of Endo Shusaku, a Roman Catholic layperson, whose lifelong struggle lies in the gap between Western Christianity and Japanese culture. See also Furuya, *History of Japanese Theology*. In chapter 1, the first generation of Protestant theologians is explored.

22. Suzuki, "Translation of God: Part Two," 146, quoting from Uemura, *Uemura Masahisa*.

In Japan, while the Protestant God was claimed to be the True Kami, as long as no other True Kami appeared to defy it, the situation was comparatively safe. But when one *kami* among the Japanese *kami* was given absolutistic character, it followed that its relationship to the Protestant's *True Kami* became a burning issue.[23]

Kitamori, a third-generation Protestant theologian in Japan, shares the direction of this protestant apologetic concern in the Japanese cultural context from the beginning.[24] He is wary that the God witnessed by the Scripture is mingled with Japanese kami in the highly religious pluralistic situation. In this regard, his theological strategy is in the same line with Uemura's "True God" apologetics mentioned above. While he avoids being captivated by the imitation of Western mission theology, he also avoids being absorbed in the polytheistic Shinto kami. Apart from the first perspective, which Kitamori shares, there is a different perspective to approach Japanese culture in terms of kami. While the first perspective is questioned from the biblical faith in Japanese culture, the second perspective comes from Japanese culture into Christian faith. While the first is the question of Christian identity, the second is an approach from the identity of local culture: Japanese identity. The latter perspective is taken up not only by Japanese Christians like Endo Shusaku, but also by other intellectuals who are concerned about the study of Japan interdisciplinarily. Some of them explore the unifying power behind the Japanese pluralistic situation.

The Original Suspicion of Christian Mission in Japan

Japanese intellectuals have been suspicious of the success of Christian mission in Japan not because of political-military confrontation but because of Japan's religious-cultural tradition. They approach the same issue that the Protestant theologians like Uemura and Kitamori struggled with as a theological issue. The original question can be traced back to *The Faint Smiles of the Gods,* written by the Japanese writer Ryunosuke Akutagawa (1892–1927). In this book, the hero is a Jesuit, Padre Organtino, whose missionary work in Japan dated from the sixteenth century and which gave him great satisfaction. Nevertheless, he was suddenly caught in an

---

23. Suzuki, "Translation of God: Part Two," 150.

24. Kitamori, "Is 'Japanese Theology' Possible?" 76–87. In order to construct "Japanese theology," Kitamori seeks a synthetic way between Uchimura and Uemura in this article.

enigmatic melancholy. One day, in a hallucination, he met an old man who represented one of the spirits of this land (Japan). The old man calmly started to talk to him about how any foreign thought, whether Buddhist or Confucian, can be changed, and then he added that the deity that Christianity brought is not exceptional. He continued to tell Organtino, who was insisting on his successful conversion efforts "ours is not the power that destroys. It is the power that recreates."[25] Finally, the old man left some words and faded away:

> However widespread Catholicism may be, you cannot say that it will certainly be victorious. . . . Perhaps Deus Himself will be transformed into a native of this land. China and India were transformed. The West too will have to be transformed. We are in the trees. And in the flow of shallow waters . . . in the wind . . . in the evening light . . . We are everywhere and always. Beware. Beware.[26]

Akutagawa's sharp insight is not directed to the "power that destroys." Rather, he ponders the *Japanese* "power that recreates" the Western Christian power. It must be noted that, although he presupposes animism, he does not identify power with the pluralistic culture as it is. He quickly moves to his own perspective in which there is something behind the appearance of animism, but the actuality is that China (Confucianism and Taoism), India (Buddhism), and the West (Christianity) are recreated. He knows that a simple form of animism is not enough to actualize the "power that recreates" these world religions historically within and out of Japan. Rather, he finds a different root behind primitive animism, but it is unspeakable. Thus, the old man just says, "Beware. Beware."

Robert Bellah: the Tradition of Submerged Transcendence

Akutagawa alludes to the origin of this creative power, not as political-military power (imperial power), but as cultural power. It is not "the power that destroys" but "the power that recreates." In any case, the question remains today. For instance, Robert Bellah, the American sociologist, is entangled with the same issue as that of Akutagawa when

---

25. Akutagawa, "Faint Smiles of the Gods," 126. The original text was published in 1922.

26. Ibid., 127.

he says, "When I spoke of the 'tradition' of submerged transcendence,' I was referring to the presence of axial traditions in Japan—Buddhist, Confucian, Christian, Marxist—that never quite succeeded in replacing the preaxial premises of Japanese culture."[27]

It is interesting to compare this quotation with Akutagawa's. As literature, Akutagawa employed a tricky rhetoric to make readers confused about the relationship between power and animism, but he eventually leaves only a scent of the real origin of power: "Beware. Beware."

On the other hand, Bellah clearly says that it is founded on the social value system.[28] According to him, Japan first imported innumerable cultural elements from China in the sixth and seventh centuries, such as a written language, classic literature, complex religion, political theory, a legal system, an elaborate bureaucracy, a coinage system, forms of land tenure, and universal religions (Buddhism and Confucianism). On the other hand, in the nineteenth and twentieth centuries, the post-Tokugawa society also imported political, legal, economic, and educational systems from the West. Once these were imported, they were indigenized and contributed to a rapid advance in structural differentiation. However, the prominent feature is the fact that these were carried "under the aegis of the emperor system by groups organized in a typically Japanese way,"[29] so that they reinforced the "particularistic central values" without threatening the value system. The Japanese have not rejected their axial, transcendent, or universal elements; "instead they have continuously revised them without abandoning them."[30] Bellah summarizes continuity and change in the face of foreign contact: "The continuity is mainly in the realm of values and the structure of group life. The change is mainly in cultural content and large-scale institutional and organizational forms."[31]

---

27. Bellah, *Imaging Japan*, 7. In this connection, "civil religion in America," which Bellah coined, was inspired from his analysis of the Japanese social value system.

28. Bellah, *Tokugawa Religion*. In his former study of Japan, Bellah's main concern was how Japan attained modernization as universal phenomena out of the Western/Christian tradition. However, after a half century, he changes the focal point from the universal dimension of modernization in Japan to the particular way to accomplish modernization in the Japanese way. While he sheds light on the history of the encounter of Japan with "axial religion/civilization," he finds a cultural pattern to dissolve the transcendent into the immanent.

29. Bellah, *Imaging Japan*, 190.

30. Ibid., 7.

31. Ibid., 191.

Again, in relation to Akutagawa, it is worth noting the above sentence, "not rejected" but "revised." The "tradition" allows anything universal/transcendental to exist in the tradition, as long as it serves to support the central values. This has prompted all universal religions (Buddhism, Confucianism, and Christianity) to be *Japanized*. When Japanese religion is limited by Japan's central values, they have provided a safety valve for the dominant system. The more the central values emphasize particular loyalty to a particular group, culminating in an emperor system in the modern imperial Japan, the more subversive universality beyond the national substance seems to be. Bellah summarizes the civil religion of Japan as a tradition of submerged transcendence: "From Buddhism to Christianity . . . Japan continues to be Asian but not Asian, Western but not Western."[32] Therefore, attempts to investigate the *essence* of Japan's culture come to an elusive deadlock. Akutagawa's voice still echoes, "Beware. Beware."

Akutagawa and Bellah both discuss conditions in which Christianity exists culturally and sociologically. It does not matter whether their attitudes were favorable to Christianity or not. Their concern is given to the inner mechanism to be "not rejected, but revised." If Akutagawa and Bellah are correct, what is "not rejected but revised" in the case of Christian God? Before returning to Kitamori, I will explore the second perspective in terms of kami translation, that of local cultural identity. It is Endo Shusaku who most honestly and existentially approaches the "power that recreates" or the "tradition of submerged transcendence" from his own faith and cultural identity. He energetically embraces the "failure" of Xavier not only as a one-sided Christian judgment but as his own cultural judgment. Lifting up Endo's search, Mase-Hasegawa understands Endo as an inculturation theologian through her theological study of his novels.[33] I will take up Endo's inculturation process by following her study of Endo and try to show the same issue, the view of God, from a different angle.

ENDO SHUSAKU: IN THE LIGHT OF *KOSHINTO* JAPAN

Endo is a unique Christian novelist who eagerly depicts the faces of Christ Asian people can recognize in his literary works. C. S. Song also

---

32. Ibid., 207.

33. Mase-Hasegawa, *Christ in Japanese Culture.*

evaluates Endo's theological contribution in that he sets up the factor of local culture as a hermeneutical device for Christian faith.[34] The common notion of Western Christianity and theology between Song and Endo is to consider them as a metaphysical-philosophical tradition that has suppressed Asian people's capacity to imagine their God and Christ in their own way. Rational theology cannot be helpful for Asian people in Song and for Japanese people in Endo because it does not touch on the ordinary people's lives. They turn over the relationship between Asian or Japanese tradition and Western tradition and reconstruct Christian faith from their own traditions.

Endo's works avoid a thematic understanding of God, and his idea is basically open-ended. He depicts the new faces of Christ in a way that makes readers deconstruct given images of Christ. Some theologians find in his method commonality with Luther's theology of the cross.[35] His concern is not directed to the cross, but to the crucified Christ. For Endo, the cross is not merely that which a believer experiences in socio-cultural conflict, in poverty, war, or injustice. The theme that Endo addresses implies the shadow of belief in Jesus Christ. His representative work, *Silence*, in which he addresses the age of persecution against Christianity in seventeenth-century Japan, alludes to Endo's sense of faith in the context of Japan. It never occurred to him to say that to believe in God/Christ is to make people happy in a simple manner.

Just as Buddhism says that life itself is suffering, Endo seems to propose that faith itself is suffering. He declines a simple dichotomy between right and wrong or between light and darkness even in terms of Christian faith. Both are inextricably and paradoxically connected to each other in his writings. He reaches a point where conventional knowledge about human life and Christian faith breaks through. The reality of life and the reality of faith converge in the encounter with Jesus Christ. The face of this Christ is unique in a way that challenges the face of Christ imposed by Western Christianity, characterized by a "paternal" and "judging" God. This alternative is the "maternal" and "embracing" God.

---

34. Song, *Third-eye Theology*, 7–10.

35. Bussie proposes the theological relevancy between Luther and Endo in terms of a theology of the cross in *aughter of the Oppressed*. The other writing is: Sundermeier, *Das Kreuz als Befreiung*.

Endo's Inculturation Process

Mase-Hasegawa divides the long career of Endo into three periods in order to fully explore Endo's work as inculturation theology: 1) conflict period: 1947–65; 2) reconciliation period: 1966–1980; and 3) mutual integration period: 1981–1993. In the first stage, Endo attempts to see the relationship between Japan and Christianity from the viewpoint of Christianity. For example, what mainly appears as a critical question in *Sea and Poison* is how Japanese people understand sin.[36] In this novel, Endo illustrates the lack of understanding of sin and guilt among the Japanese from the viewpoint of the universal doctrine of sin. He demonstrates the correlation between the lack of understanding sin and guilt and the deficiency of a transcendent God. For Endo, this is the main reason why the Japanese do not accept Christianity. Moving to the second stage, Endo continued to have protagonists ask difficult questions about the Japanese inability to accept Christianity. In *Silence*, for instance, Ferreira, the apostate who worked as a missionary for twenty years, speaks to his former student:

> This country is a more terrible swamp . . . we have planted the sapling of Christianity in this swamp . . . supposing the God whom those Japanese believed in was not the God of Christian teaching.[37]

Saying so, the difficulty of the translation for the name of God that Xavier confronted was inscribed in their hearts:

> From the beginning those same Japanese who confused "Deus" and "Dainishi" twisted and changed our God and began to create something different. Even when the confusion of vocabulary disappeared the twisting and changing secretly continued. . . . Japanese did not believe in the Christian God but in their own distortion.[38]

He eventually professes from his own experience: "Japanese till this day have never had the concept of God; and they never will."[39] Here, he represents the attribution of Japanese culture rather than the issue of theology in terms of the translation of the name of God. There is no

---

36. Endo, *The Sea and Poison*.
37. Endo, *Silence*, 147.
38. Ibid., 148.
39. Ibid., 147.

one other than Endo who presents the harsh reality of Christianity in Japan since Xavier came. Sooner or later, Christians in Japan come to the same point that they confronted. Nevertheless, Endo comes to an epistemological turn in this second stage. Mase-Hasegawa calls it the "reconciliation" period. What reconciles what? It is not easy to specify. When the hero, the last priest in the country, is about to apostatize, Christ in bronze speaks to him, "Trample! Trample! I more than anyone know of the pain in your foot. Trample! It was to be trampled on by men that I was born into this world."[40]

Silence, the work that has brought about a great deal of controversy, expresses Endo's discovery of Christ in the swamp of Japan. The epistemological turn changes the direction of his questions like, "What kind of Christianity makes Endo feel that Japanese are deficient?" That is Western institutionalized Christianity. From the viewpoint of Western Christianity, Japanese people cannot understand their traditional understanding of God, sin, and death. But Christ comes to the protagonists in a different way than what they teach. Endo came to the conviction that the Japanese can meet Christ without Western Christianity. It is a different kind of reconciliation between Japanese and Christianity. The image of Christ functions to suspend the move from the conflict period to the reconciliation. Endo's Christology offers an antithesis to the Western Christology: against "truiumphalistic," "paternal," and "heroic" images of Christ. It is Endo's kenotic Christology in the second stage that many western theologians pay attention to. They find in Endo a new perspective on Christian faith, Christology, and missiology, which provides for post-Christendom Christianity.[41] Their agreement with Endo is the Jesus who was crucified as "weak, suffered, and died in all his agony."[42] Unlike Kitamori, Endo vigorously seeks the face of Jesus in the midst of human ineffectiveness.

In the third period of Endo's literary life, the "mutual integration period (1981–1993)," Mase-Hasegawa argues that Endo's Christ and God come to be harmonized into the *koshinto* spirituality. According to her study, the topics that had preoccupied Endo, like human sinfulness, guilt, and God's judgment, weakened as Western Christianity constructions. On the other hand, his concern clings to focus on the rhythm between life

---

40. Ibid., 171.

41. See Hoekema, "The 'Christology' of Shusaku Endo," 230–48; Matsuoka, "The Church in the World," 294–9.

42. Mase-Hasegawa, "Image of Christ for Japanese," 27.

and death, in which people discover a spiritual force. His final work, *Deep River*, seeks not only to deepen his understanding of Christ but also to radicalize the Christian God into an emptying God. For him, one does not need to claim any difference between religions and between the names of God. The love of God is in the presence of all living people, like the wind and river. All are embraced by the great love, like the Ganges River embraces the living and the dead. Endo depicts the embracing God, who suffers and empties himself because of the embracing love.

One of the main characters, who was filled with the agony of her life and came to India, happened to see two young nuns going to take a dying woman from off of the street in front of her. She asked them honestly, "Why are you doing this?"[43] The nuns slowly answered her, "Because except for this . . . there is nothing in this world that we can believe in."[44] After hearing this reply, her consideration is more important: "Her words for 'this' do not describe clearly what she means. If the nun had said 'Only Him,' then she means Ootsu's Onion, Jesus Christ. But she does not signify whether 'this' is personal or impersonal."[45] The Christ can be incarnated into the protagonist, who failed the official teaching of the Roman Catholics, into the Hindu goddess *Chamunda*, and into the Ganges River, which represents the mother of India. That is the "pneumatological Christ" that she names the third period's Christology of Endo. The personhood of Jesus Christ still remains there. Jesus remains within the memory of people, but the real presence of Christ is inscribed within the life of people: the "all-embracing spirit of love is emphasized, which Christ embodies . . . the love of God reaches each individual and awakens his/her spirituality. It is God's universal action."[46] Christ is selfless love as thoroughly as he loses his particular name. God is not being. God should be expressed with verbs. Endo shapes his belief into his Asian faces of Christ in this way. Endo eventually develops the kenosis Christ into the nameless/faceless Christ and radicalizes the cross to a point where the cross is completely dissolved into people's experience of life.

When Christ comes to this spiritual Christ in a pluralist context, Mase-Hasegawa insists on the koshinto-understanding of "spiritual-

---

43. Endo, *Deep River*, 215, quoted in Mase-Hasegawa, "Image of Christ for Japanese," 30.

44. Mase-Hasegawa, "Image of Christ for Japanese," 30.

45. Ibid.

46. Mase-Hasegawa, *Christ in Japanese Culture*, 159.

ity": "The Japanese and western frameworks for experiencing and understanding 'spirit' apparently differ. The former framework is largely animistic and pantheistic, and the latter is informed by biblical monotheistic traditions."[47] The main thesis of her study is that the goal of Endo's inculturation is accomplished in order to be compatible with *koshinto* spirituality. She comes to the same issue of kami as the Protestant theologians from the different perspective through the study of Endo, the perspective of local cultural identity.

Koshinto

Koshinto is the prototype of Shinto, the Japanese folk religion. According to Mase-Hasegawa, the term koshinto is an analytical construction that scholars created in the modern age to clarify the "core element of Japanese culture prior to 300 BC."[48] While Shinto makes it possible for people to worship an innumerable number of deities, koshinto did not worship gods or goddesses; rather, the objects of worship were the "power of spirit."[49] Her hypothesis is that "koshinto is the living spiritual root of the Japanese people and that it continues to play an important role in Japanese self understanding."[50] Following this thesis, she supposes that the inculturation process revealed in Endo's literature is a transformation of Western Christianity into that which conforms to koshinto spirituality. She presents six features of the meaning of kami (gods) in Shinto study:

1. Kami are not monotheistic but polytheistic beings
2. Kami do not have a concrete form or shape
3. Kami float, move, wander, and sometimes cling to people
4. Kami dictate and rule each place and substance
5. Kami are fearful natural deities
6. Kami are anthropomorphic deities[51]

---

47. Ibid., 176–7.
48. Ibid., 7. It is said that koshinto is traced back prior to 300 BC. The word shinto first appeared in the *Nihon-Shoki* (AD 720).
49. Ibid., 18.
50. Ibid., 29.
51. Ibid., 30. Cf. Suzuki, "Translation of God: Part One," 139–42. Suzuki introduces the debates about the translation for God in China's mission context in the nineteenth

The perception of kami in koshinto does not rely on a rational consistency but on an empirical feeling on the basis of animism. The god(s) are not transcendent and omnipotent beings. They have no shape or form. In addition, kami have no distinction between singular and plurality. Rather, she says, "Japanese *kami* are considered as a life force within all beings."[52] As long as she stands on this definition, she does not distinguish *pantheism* and *pan-en-theisim*. Both seem to be possible, given her explanation. From her analysis of the inculturation into koshinto kami, she concludes that Endo's Christian faith, which was once obsessed with Western Christianity, is inculturated into the koshinto spirituality. Once he is anchored in koshinto, she argues, his Christianity opens to a universal dimension in the aspect of experience. My focal point is that she presents Christian kami, which is compatible with koshinto kami, through her theological analysis of Endo's literary works.

First, the Christian kami as well as the koshinto kami is an all-embracing deity that does not distinguish between the strong and the weak or between the rich and the poor or between the orthodox and the heretic in her study. There is no distinction in this theological parameter. Second, the Christian kami is the "maternal deity" that never judges the sin and evil of human beings, forgives everything and everyone, and accompanies us beyond the distinction of life and death. Third, the Christian kami does not contradict the universal spirits that pervade into other religions and creatures pantheistically and panentheistically.

In comparison with Kitamori's theology of the pain of God, I find both commonality and difference. First of all, Kitamori and Endo both have an aesthetic way of approaching God. Otto criticizes Kitamori about this point because he seems to think that Kitamori betrays the biblical message:

---

century. Protestant missionaries had a great deal of controversy about whether God was translated in to *Shangdi* or *Shen*. *Shen* is the Chinese pronunciation of Japanese *kami*. W. H. Medhurst, one of leading missionaries for Bible translation, proposed eight arguments to explain the inappropriateness of *Shen* for the translation for God: 1) *Shen* does not carry the sense of a magnificent being; 2) *Shen* is equivalent to the English *spirit*; 3) *Shen* is not necessarily the object to be worshiped; 4) *Shen* could be a good as well as a bad being; 5) *Shen* was used to denote the *spirit* of humans, not a *god*; 6) *Shen* cannot distinguish the Creator God from the ancestors' spirits; 7) because *Shen* is equivalent to *spirit* in Chinese, there is no distinction between *Shen*-God and *Shen*-spirit; 8) the Roman Catholics have already used *shen* as the translation for *spirit*.

52. Ibid., 31.

Kitamori's theology, moreover, must be categorized as aesthetical. ... no question that Japanese thought in general, and Buddhist religion, in particular, inform Kitamori's theological formulations. Intuition in Buddhism is a fundamental experience of immediate, unreflective perception which knows no objectification and no methods. It is pure experience, beyond space and time, having nothing to do with the discursive reasoning so prominent in Western thought.[53]

Although Otto ascribes Japanese aestheticism to Buddhism, Mase-Hasegawa argues that this can be traced back to koshinto spirituality that is older and more fundamental than Buddhism in Japanese cultural formation. Otto continues to criticize Kitamori in that Kitamori's aesthetics sets aside "faith and belief" as doctrinal elements, and just "pays lip service to the idea of the Son as a substitutionary sacrifice."[54] He argues that these things are the consequence of his being "nationalistically-oriented" and his "tendency toward syncretism, or synthesis," which leaves him irresponsible for the judgment between good and evil, between faith and unbelief.[55] He concludes, "Kitamori's theology of the pain of God is based primarily on Japanese religious motifs, not on Scripture."[56] On the other hand, Carl Michalson positively evaluates Kitamori in that he uses the aesthetics of suffering (pain: tsurasa) that enable the Japanese to link "God, Christian faith and Japanese existence."[57] Reflecting on koshinto's "all-embracing principle" with the six methodological features, Kitamori's way of theology almost overlaps this principle.[58] It is right to say that Kitamori also argues for the all-embracing God in his theology of the pain of God. However, I find a subtle but decisive difference between Kitamori and koshinto. While Kitamori recognizes the importance that Endo projects on the transformation from the "paternal religion" of Christianity to the "maternal religion," he insists that his own

---

53. Otto, "Japanese Religion in *Theology of the Pain*," 40.
54. Ibid., 43.
55. Ibid., 40.
56. Ibid., 43.
57. Michalson, "Theology of the Pain," 74.
58. Mase-Hasegawa, *Christ in Japanese Culture*, 44. She proposes six features of koshinto theology: 1) syncretistic-synthetic; 2) harmony oriented; 3) emotional, not rational; 4) loyalty to nature; 5) the mental structure of *amae*; 6) feminine dimension of the divine: "maternal worldview is to acknowledge everything as it is, forgive and accept."

project is how to integrate these oppositional features into the element of the gospel message.[59]

According to Kitamori, the pain of God is not directed to compassion for the weak. Following Paul's theology of the cross, Kitamori emphasizes the double notion of a human being. That is, a human being is not only weak (Rom 5:6) but also the enemy (Rom 5:10). He cannot overlook the combination of being weak with the enemy because it is connected to overlooking the gospel, which states, "Christ died for us while we were still enemies."[60] This is the focal point of the theology of the pain of God. The reaction of God to sin is the wrath of God, not compassion. However, the wrath of God cannot be directed to the punishment of God or the expiation in satisfaction theory. If Otto believes that the punishment or compensation is only biblical, his criticism is right.

Kitamori himself deviates from atonement, which confronts human beings with punishment and compensation. The wrath of God is imposed on Christ. It is the pain of God: the Father let the Son die, and the Son suffers the death of the cross. Therefore, in the case of Kitamori, pain represents the Trinitarian suffering of the cross, which alone reveals the all-embracing love of God for sinners, even when God could not embrace, forgive, and love. It is the paradoxical connection between the sinful reality of human beings and the infinitely embracing reality of God. Kitamori's theology of the pain of God takes the form of a double negation to come to affirmation. That is why Kitamori recognizes that Endo's maternal God is the God without the cross. In the case of Endo, the maternal God has no dilemma regarding the weak and the enemy. There is no enemy against Christ without conflict. This is the kami context in the "tradition of submerged transcendence" that Kitamori confronts.

EXPANSION OF THE PERSPECTIVE OF GOD IN THE JAPANESE CONTEXT

In this context of kami, Kitamori repeatedly emphasizes that "theology is ultimately the view of God." It leads him to speak about the essence of God through his theology of the cross. He attempts to clarify the absolute other through the cross, which confronts human beings and at

---

59. Kitamori, *Urei naki kami*, 304–40.
60. Ibid., 308.

the same time embraces. Onodera Isao, a Roman Catholic theologian, understands Kitamori in relation with the Trinitarian theologian:

> [For Kitamori,] the content of Christ's cross is the harmonization of contradictions between the wrath of God and the love of God or between Law and Gospel. This is both two and one. Not until knowing the Trinitarian background of Kitamori can we understand the vivid significance of the theology of the pain of God. The love rooted in the pain of God as synthesis enhances itself from the cross of Christ through the resurrection into the love of Holy Spirit.[61]

According to Onodera, when Kitamori was seventeen years old, he first read the Bible. He immediately understood the relationship between the Father and himself, but he did not realize the significance of Christ for a while. Following the order of love that Kitamori would later develop, he stayed at the first order of love: the immediate love of the Father in the pure relationship with Christ. There was no room for Christ as a mediator between the Father and sinners. However, his faith was shortly wrecked when he realized himself as the one who was left out of divine providence and who was in trouble because of his egocentrism. Kitamori confessed later that he came to encounter Christ the savior "who saves up the forsaken" instead of the God of providence.[62]

Onodera reports that Kitamori was led to Luther's justification by faith in those days and experienced "passive repentance." The transition from trust in the immediate love of God through the loss of trust into faith in Christ led Kitamori to open his eyes to the paradoxical love of God who embraces the wrecked sinner. God is not a simple monotheistic deity to swing between the god who judges the bad and the god who favors the good. God does not overlook sin, injustice, and evil and at the same time, solves them in his own way. Here, the distinction between Endo's "maternal" deity and Kitamori's synthesis between "paternal" and "maternal" deities appears. Endo came to the maternal God by casting away the paternal God. The paternal God that Endo finds is the Western Christian God and the one who does not overlook sin and punishes sinners. On the other hand, the maternal God attends to the agony, weakness, and regret of sinners. Endo never neglects the existence of human sinfulness and evilness. However, that the maternal God relates to sin-

61. Onodera, *Zettaimu to Kami*, 259–60.
62. Ibid., 255–6, quoting from Kitamori, *Shingaku teki jiden I*.

ners points to the dark side of sinners. Because of sinners' weakness and agony, God embraces them in spite of their sinfulness. God never questions the sin that they commit. Christ touches the weakness of sinners. Christ cannot be related to the solution of sin, because God cannot relate to justice. What Christ can engage in is compassion for the weakness of sinners. Once God relates to justice, he cannot help but judge them in a sense of punishment. Therefore, Endo does not find any comfort with the paternality of God.

This paternal deity is equivalent to the God of providence by which Kitamori was depressed in his youth. While Endo identifies the paternal God with the Western construction of God, Kitamori understands this God as the God of providence or law in the Scripture. From here, their paths to the gospel differ. Regarding Luther's theology, God is the God of law. It is persuasive to say that Endo's maternal God is compatible with koshinto spirituality, as Mase-Hasegawa clearly proposes. Probably Kitamori does not reject this contribution. However, the issue that Kitamori relates himself to is different from Endo. It is the integration between the law of God and the gospel of God by using a Hegelian synthesis. Going through the synthesis between law and the gospel, Kitamori comes to meet the God of pain rooted in love.

This is not relevant to Christian monism but is rather Trinitarian. Therefore, Onodera finds the traces of Trinitarian thought in Kitamori's theology. For Trinitarian theology, the choice of the maternal God over the paternal God is the other side of monotheism. Judgment cannot be entangled with the punishment or satisfaction that the traditional monotheism overemphasizes. Rather, the dimension of law and judgment opens us to the otherness of God and the justice of God. Kitamori ponders the otherness and justice of God in a Trinitarian way, though he shows the limitation from the contemporary development of Trinitarian justice and otherness. Michalson has already realized Kitamori's accent of the Trinity in his theology of the pain of God: "It is revolutionary chiefly to those who, like Karl Barth, have espoused an immanental view of the Trinity. This is the view of the Trinity that defines God's threeness in terms of relations within the Godhead."[63]

In saying that the essence of God is pain, Kitamori prioritizes the Father letting the Son die over the Father begetting the Son. Kitamori's task is to bring back the cross of Christ into the Trinity. The incarnation

---

63. Michalson, "Theology of the Pain," 90.

of Christ means that the divinity of Christ goes outside himself. The "going outside" makes it possible to include human beings who are wrecked: "The pain of God is nothing but the outsideness of God's selfsameness."[64] From here, it becomes apparent that Kitamori is different from patripassianism, which cannot separate the Son from the Father in its unification of divinity. Kitamori insists that God goes outside himself only in the person of the Son. The Son suffers by going outside himself, and the Father suffers by the Son's outsideness. "Going outside" means the Trinitarian pain of God. The cross is related in the essence of God in the Trinitarian form.

God's Pain in the View of Eternity

The second most astonishing biblical passage to Kitamori is Hebrews 2:10: "It was fitting that God, for whom and through whom all things exist, in bringing many children to glory, should make the pioneer of their salvation perfect through sufferings." It makes him feel as if the entire universe would be shaken. This impact leads him to avoid the framework of the traditional atonement interpretation of the death of Christ: "In a church that has lost this wonder, unastonishing theological doctrines teach that God, against his nature, took an emergency measure and made Christ suffer for the redemption of sin."[65] When he reads the small word "fitting" as necessary to God, it convinces him that the cross is not read by the way of cause and effect between human sin and compensation. Rather, he starts looking at the death of Christ as the event within God from eternity. The pain of God is part of his essence. Therefore, he continues to say that the "cross is in no sense an external act of God, but an act within himself."[66] He understands the mystery of incarnation from the cross event. From the cross as an act of God within himself, Kitamori looks into the mystery of incarnation—that is, that "the 'Father begets the Son' is secondary to the primary words 'the Father causes his Son to die.'"[67] That God embraces sinners is consistent with the work of God from eternity. He understands the incarnation of the Son as "going outside him." It is the proto-cross event. However,

---

64. Ibid., 91.
65. Kitamori, *Theology of the Pain*, 45.
66. Ibid., 45.
67. Ibid., 47.

the realization of this is the historical cross. The cross sheds light on the eternal pain of God—the eternal decision of the Father embracing all.

The relational concept of pain between the Father and the Son presents two aspects of God's pain. The one is "the pain of God reflects his heart, loving those who should not be loved" and the second is "the pain of God reflects his heart, allowing his only Son to die."[68] The latter happened for the former. The death of the Son is the consequence of the completion of the principle of embracement. Thus, his accent does not lie in the substitution nor the satisfaction. It is certain that Kitamori holds firmly to the wrath of God as the reaction to sin. However, as Michalson points out, the wrath of God is not imposed on sinners as punishment or compensation. The synthesis between discontinuity and continuity in the relationship between God and sinners is everything for Kitamori. The historical cross of Jesus functions to reveal the Father's heart. From here, he introduces the aesthetic way of tsurasa in Japanese kabuki drama. Everything, including Christology, converges on the first article of the creed to indicate the pain-filled heart of the Father.[69]

I believe that the theology of the pain of God helps me find the particular context of talk about God. First, the view of God that Kitamori tackles is similar but alien to the koshinto spirituality that Endo's inculturation theology resonates with. If Mase-Hasegawa's hypothesis is right that koshinto is Japanese spirituality, the theology of the pain of God cannot be said to be "Japanese," though it is still an oversimplification to say that the opposite of "Japanese" is the "Western imitation." Rather, for Kitamori, the sustainability of sin and the wrath of God as the reaction to sin serves to reveal the wholly other. The absolute other is different from the Greek impassible and unchangeable deity. The absolute other is the God of love, who has a yearning heart to seek the lost one. The cross of Jesus Christ gives a double reality to pain: the Father's pain and our pain. Human pain is an epistemological point of contact with the heart of God in a paradoxical manner. Kitamori sees the reality of sin not as the reality outside God but as the reality inside God. This does not mean legalistic forgiveness. It points to God's embracing character in the midst of the reality of rejection. He enhances loving the enemy from an ethical commandment to making it into a view of God. The love of God

---

68. Ibid., 90.

69. Sundermeier, *Das Kreuz als Befreiung*, 87: "Die Christologie wird in den ersten Glaubensartikel aufgesogen."

is not immediate love but the love that embraces outside love. He follows the double view of the anthropology of Pauline theology, seeing both weakness and enmity. Jesus Christ, who responds to both dimensions, accompanies mankind thoroughly, even if a human being sins against, betrays, and forsakes him.

From the viewpoint of Kitamori, there is no cross in the Jesus who just accompanies the weak because there is no difference between God, Jesus, and the weak in quality. They can be tied by natural love, like maternal love for children. On the other hand, Kitamori sticks to the other side of the weak. The weak can be offensive for Christ because of selfishness or being self-bound. The reaction to sin is the wrath of God. When the wrath of God comes into a theological perspective, it points to the otherness of God. While Kitamori sustains the existence of immediate love between the Father and the Son, he assures that it is discontinued with human beings because of human sinfulness. Accepting that otherness is bound to sinfulness, pain happens. The acceptance is not the acceptance of similarity but the acceptance of difference. Therefore, the cross is the symbol of the acceptance of differentiation with the mediation of pain. As long as one stands on this embracing principle, the atonement cannot be connected principally with compensation or punishment. This is the reason why those who understand his theology in the framework of traditional atonement theories evaluate his theology as a deviation from their tradition. To Kitamori, the absurdity is not theodicy but loving the enemy. Although Kitamori does not fully develop the idea, the acceptance of difference arises.

Second, challenging the impassibility of God, Kitamori attempts to go beyond the framework of atonement theory and see pain in the immanent Trinity. It is expressed by the relational concept of pain, which discloses the pain with the Trinity from eternity. The cross of the Son and human sin are not reduced into a straight relationship of cause and effect. Kitamori's emphasis is on the all-embracing God, even if human beings transgress, sin, and go outside the grace of God. The foundation of the all-embracing concept is not compassion but the Trinitarian decision from eternity that the Father let the Son die on the cross. There is dissonance between the historical cross and the Cross of Christ in the Trinity. Just as Victor Raj points out, there is both the "heart of God" of the cross and the "action of the cross" in Kitamori.[70] The first is distin-

---

70. Raj, "The Pain of God," 28.

guishable from the latter, and the meaning of the first also absorbs that of the second. As a consequence, there is little space to consider the meaning of the historical cross itself in his theology. Paul Chung argues that Kitamori is bound to the Father letting the Son die, and he fails to clarify the unselfish love of the Son embodied in Jesus. This failure results in the absence of a cosmic dimension in his theology of the pain of God. Chung sheds light on the immanent Trinity from the unselfish-voluntary love of the Son from eternity. I will explore this point in chapter 5.

I will shift my focus to other Asian theologies of the cross. There are some who approach Kitamori's theology of the cross from their own contextual theologies of the cross. They find both a contribution and deficiency in theology of the pain of God. I will explore how the other theologians of the cross understand Kitamori in the Asian context. As long as Japanese culture shares Asian religiosity, there should be something relevant. In addition, considering the fact that Kitamori leaves no trace of taking up a dialogue with other Asian theologians, their voices are necessary to rethink his theology. That is the task of the inter-contextual reading of the cross.

RESPONSE TO PAIN IN THE CONTEXT OF SUFFERING

C. S. Song

Song is a provocative theologian who proposes an Asian political theology. His main concern is how Asian people can meet the "God of compassion." But he does not mean that Asian people must encounter a Christian God outside of their traditions, because they have lots of stories that convince them that God loves them both before and after they encounter Christianity.[71] The important thing is that Asian people "must train themselves to see Christ through Chinese eyes, Japanese eyes, Asian eyes, African eyes, Latin American eyes."[72] According to Song, the God that Christian theologians traditionally have suggested is the "God of retribution." It is this God Job objected to and his friends urged him to obey. It is this God who delivered Jesus onto the cross and into death, who demanded his blood and was satisfied with his death. This God also approves of violence and sacrifice and permits bloodshed and war in the world. Those theologians who have upheld such a God

71. Song, *Theology from the Womb of Asia*, 126–7.
72. Song, *Third-eye Theology*, 11.

could allow Christianity to join hands with colonialism. Song calls on the oppressed people to discard the false god traditional theologians invent and then to restore the true God who Jesus called "Abba." This God is synonymous with "the God of compassion" (*Theology from the Womb of Asia*) and "the father of the prodigal son" (*Third-eye Theology*). When Jesus cried on the cross, "My God, my God, why hast thou forsaken me," it is interpreted as "the cry of a love that has been injured and crucified but does not give up."[73] He does not accept any theological meaning like atonement theories in the cross. For Song, the cross is nothing other than a tragedy, as he argues:

> The cross is the suffering of Jesus of Nazareth and it is the suffering of humanity. The cross means human being rejecting human beings. It is human beings abandoning human beings. It shows how human beings in the grips of demonic powers, are inflicting injustice on each other, tearing each other apart, destroying each other . . . It was not conspired by Jesus' Abba-God, but by the God invented by the religious authorities.[74]

Accordingly, the cross of Jesus is only the death of one person, who had a pure belief in Abba-God and people. Abba-God has spoken silent words to human beings in horror, grief, and protest, "What have you human beings done to Jesus, 'my beloved son'?"[75] Abba-God not only maintained silence but also prepared to receive the life and death of Jesus into God's womb. Here, Song creatively combines the biblical story of the cross and resurrection with Buddhism's *karuna*:

> It (God's silence at the cross) must be pity, *karuna*, the matrix, the womb, engaged in the creation of life and nourishment of it . . . That silence of God is like a womb enveloping Jesus on the cross, empowering him during the last moments of his life and nourishing him for the resurrection of a new life from the tomb.[76]

His theology of the cross is not related to any doctrine, but at the same time, it is always connected with the salvation of all people in light of Asian folk tales and stories about the compassion of God. Not only Jesus but also all human beings come from the womb of God and then

---

73. Song, *Theology from the Womb of Asia*, 67.
74. Song, *Jesus, the Crucified People*, 99.
75. Ibid., 114–6.
76. Ibid., 119.

return there. God is the origin of life. All people can be welcome to the love and pity of God. Song does not need Christology as a mediator because people are the mediators of God. The event of the cross represents one example of how God does not and cannot leave anyone, even when he or she experiences desperate human violence, cruelty, and death. The difference between Kitamori and Song becomes clear now.

Song evaluates Kitamori in that he pioneers the use of the sensibility of local people in order to clarify the biblical message. However, he rejects Kitamori's understanding of the cross as a divine event. Song's criticism concentrates on Kitamori's focus on the wrath of God. The point is that when the wrath of God is absolutized, salvation is internalized within God. As a result, it means that salvation is accomplished within the divinity, and then it is too theological and unfamiliar to poor sinners. It makes human beings just "spectators in the salvation drama."[77] Song concludes that, when Kitamori puts himself in line with the Western theological tradition, Lutheran tradition in particular, he betrays his sensibility to Japanese spirituality.[78]

Andrew Park

Andrew Sung Park develops a theology of *han* to reconcile the massive and accumulative suffering of people with the suffering of God. From the viewpoint of salvation of victims, he criticizes the point that the salvation of sinners is not only unhelpful but also even harmful for victims. A theology of han is not a metaphor of suffering but is substantial. It is not individual but corrective in the sense that han has been accumulated from one generation to another. He argues that the original han is a more horrible reality than the doctrine of original sin.[79] Considering these critiques, the theology of han implies a great deal of criticism of the theology of the pain of God.

Just as Bonhoeffer says, "Only the suffering God can help," Park says that only the God who experiences han can save the people who take han. He clearly distinguishes the victims of han from the victimizer (sinner) and concentrates on the salvation of victims. The suffering God

---

77. Song, *Third-eye Theology*, 61.

78. Ibid., 61.

79. Park, *The Wounded Heart of God*, 72–81. Park explains that original han is transmitted into one generation by another *biologically, mentally* or *spiritually, socially,* and *racially.*

is the God for victims. Park's God overlaps with the God that Kitamori and Endo try to show in the motif of all embracement. However, what Kitamori and Endo do not fully consider is that the consequence of sin, betrayal, or abandonment is not merely self-devastation whereby the consequence of the sin or weakness comes back to one's own existential or psychological devastation or agony. For regardless of how much they depict people's agonizing situations, their theological scheme returns to the individually existential solution between one God and one sinner or coward. Park confronts this aspect of theology as being for sinners because the consequence of human sin comes to the other in this world. Viewed from the perspective of han, the salvation of both sinners and the weak is the salvation of Cain. Unless the salvation of Cain does not take into consideration the cry of Abel from under the world, the salvation is too selfish. There is no salvation of Cain without that of Abel.

Han is a wound of the heart generated by psychosomatic repression and by social, political, economic, and cultural oppression.[80] Park advances his theological exploration on the basis of "the pain of the victims of sin." This brings about a dual question concerning the doctrine of sin: the relevance and effectiveness of this doctrine for today's world, which is full of suffering: "child abuse, human rights violations, crimes of corporations, animal cruelty, and environmental crises."[81] He asks whether traditional soteriology responding to the doctrine of sin really reveals salvation among contemporary people. His answer is no, because the "traditional doctrine of sin has been one-sided, seeing the world from the perspective of the sinner only while failing to take account of the victims of sin and injustice."[82] As long as traditional soteriology focuses on salvation from sin, it functions as the salvation of sinners but not for that of victims. Therefore, he asserts that traditional soteriology must take han as a complementary concept seriously.[83]

The emphasis on the salvation of victims leads Park to talk about the han of God. He argues that God is the God who carries God's own han: the wounded heart of God. By the same token, God needs salvation to heal his own wound; the cross "is not only the symbol of God's inten-

---

80. Ibid., 10.
81. Ibid., 9.
82. Ibid., 10.
83. Ibid., 73.

tion to save humanity, but also the symbol of God's need for salvation."[84] Therefore, salvation is not framed by savior-the saved. It is framed by a more mutual relationship in terms of emancipation from han, because han can be dissolved only by han.

Park criticizes Kitamori when he says that "the pain of God is not a 'concept of substance'—it is a 'concept of relation,' a nature of 'God's love.'"[85] Kitamori insists in this sentence that the pain of God is the mediating function of God's love, not that it is not related to the substance of God. This is unacceptable for Park, who connects the suffering God with the embodied suffering of victims. God's grace is nothing but that God takes this han. Viewing the embodied suffering of han, he judges that theology of the pain of God is far removed from the embodiment of suffering and the cross.

Kosuke Koyama

I finally take up Koyama as the one who develops a theology of the cross in Asian missional context. He tries to approach Luther's theology of the cross through Kitamori's theology of the pain of God and the theology of the pain of God through Luther's theology of the cross in his Asian missiology. Koyama believes that the wrath of God, which confronts sinners in Luther and Kitamori's theology of the cross, carries an insight for Asian people, though he is keenly aware of how difficult and even harmful it is to use this idea in Asian context.[86] He finds the context introduced by the polar idea between wrath and love in Kitamori's theology of the cross. Both *tsutumu* (to wrap or embrace) and *tsurasa* (bitter feeling), which Kitamori uses as the hermeneutical key words, are familiar words to Japanese people. However, it is noteworthy that Kitamori combines both terms, embracing and feeling bitter. People know the tsutumu love (embracing love) as their life experience and also know the tsurasa (bitter feeling) as the feeling to be endured for the valued one. However,

---

84. Ibid., 121.

85. Ibid., 117, quoting from the preface to the fifth edition of *Theology of the Pain*, 16.

86. Koyama, *Water Buffalo Theology*, 53–55. He introduces his bitter experience when he preached to Thai people about Luther's "strong faith" in the midst of his spiritual struggle (Anfechtung). He tried to give a message of trusting God in spite of God's strong rejection in the interpretation of Matthew 15:21–28: "My audience went home with the impression that some kind of neurosis constitutes the vital part of the Christian faith."

they are not familiar, and they are even uncomfortable, with love that combines both tsutumu and tsurasa. While each word is very "natural" and "usual" for their life experience, the combination is "unnatural" and "unusual." Koyama positively evaluates Kitamori's theology to enhance the "unnatural" and "unusual" nature of the gospel. He asserts that God brings the unnatural-unusual love into us, who are familiar with loving "our people." In saying so, Koyama emphasizes the affirmation through negation in order to accommodate to an Asian-missiological context.[87] However, when he specifically directs the theology of the cross into Japanese context, the tension between affirmation and negation weighs toward an emphasis on the motif of negation. Koyama's theology of the cross tries to expose the idols existing in the culture: "When the cosmological embraces us there would be no judgment implied. But when the eschatological embraces, there is judgment."[88]

In his preface to *Mount Fuji and Mount Sinai*, he sets up his theology of the cross as a critical theology, that which "can really level a sharp and, at the same time, helpful critique against idolatry . . . One of the fundamental functions of theology is to expose idolatry."[89] Idolatry, which has a human-cultural-religious matrix, leads people to destruction. Human beings happen to adore false gods anywhere. A theology of the cross confronts them by reason of concentrating on "the broken Christ." One of the particular contexts that Koyama takes into consideration is "the cosmological Shinto Japan and the eschatological Christian Germany,"[90] which caused tremendous devastation during World War II, because of their self-deification.

According to Koyama, the Japanese religious tendency is circular, not linear. Salvation can be found in the circular, natural things within the world (the immanent world). For instance, he explains that a salvation model in Psalms, "help from the Lord who made heaven and earth," is turned into "our help from heaven and earth" in this tradition. Transcendence is submerged into immanence. The immanence that does not allow for transcendence makes for a circular way of thinking. It has no beginning or end. Koyama calls this tradition "cosmological."

---

87. See Koyama, *Water Buffalo Theology*, 82–89.
88. Koyama, *Mount Fuji and Mount Sinai*, 251.
89. Ibid., x.
90. Ibid., 240.

In the last century, the imperial spirit of Japan was connected with the immanent god of the emperor without transcendence. His theology of the cross confronts this immanent idol who rejects any transcendental being beyond its own immanence. The image of "the broken Christ" confronts the idol who behaves as perfect and strong. The broken Christ saves others but cannot save himself. That is the criterion of the theology of the cross. The confrontation by the broken Christ gives a critique to "the Asian cosmological mind," which tends to embrace everything indiscriminately. He suggests possibility of a "new combination of the eschatological embracing us."[91] It means affirmation through negation. I observe that Koyama tries to put the theology of the cross within the context of Asian mission and develops the theology of the cross into a critical theology to confront the idol in the Japanese context. In doing so, while Koyama continues to learn from theology of the pain of God, he transforms it into Christocentric "neighborology."

Intercontextual Evaluation of the Theology of the Pain of God

The theological orientation that Song presents, which is compatible with Endo's existential inculturation method, has commonality with Kitamori in that the suffering of God functions as an interpretive key for theologizing. The passibility of God does not matter for any of them. God is passible in suffering because of God's all-embracing love. They also share willingness to use the experience and sensibility of local people. Regarding the view of God, all of them—Kitamori, Endo, Song, Park, and Koyama—are aiming to depict the character of the all embracing. In spite of these common grounds, they differ in their interpretations of the cross, suffering, and Christ.

In general, it is not easy for them to link atonement theories with their experience and sensibility. Although Kitamori assumes the Christian tradition of the death of Christ as atonement, his theology reveals a subtle ambiguity in this point. On the one hand, it is severely criticized by those, like Otto, who believe the atonement of Christ is a centerpiece of faith. On the other hand, he is also criticized by those who find it as the arrogant discourse of Christianity, which makes innocent people feel guilty.[92] Other Asian theologians are suspicious of the au-

---

91. Ibid., 251.

92. Takizawa, "Reflection upon *Theology of the Pain*," 132. Takizawa presents one of most critical articles of theology of the pain of God. According to him, Kitamori

thenticity of the atonement theories, at least the satisfaction theory, for mission in Asia. These different understandings of atonement theories lead them to different understandings of suffering. For Kitamori, human suffering is just an epistemological point of contact with the pain of God, only in a paradoxical way. In this remark, Kitamori is criticized as if his theology is alien to Asian or Japanese sensibilities. Thus, Song completely corrects Kitamori's love of God rooted in pain into the "pain rooted in love." Finally, like Kitamori, the others think of Jesus's cross as that which carries the knowledge of God, but Christ is not necessarily a savior. In the Asian context, Christology is a counterpoint in the dialogue with Christian tradition.[93]

When the theology of the pain of God encounters the Korean theology of han, it meets a fundamental criticism. When Park finds a fundamental failure in the traditional soteriology of sinners, it should be directed to the theology of the pain of God. Although Song and Park point out that there is no room for political theology to occur in the theology of the pain of God, more importantly, it causes the pain of God to become irrelevant to the embodiment of suffering of people. Park questions if theology of the pain of God retains its embodiment of suffering. For Kitamori, the suffering of Jesus in his life and death converges on the function of the Son who witnesses the pain of the Father. In this regard, while Koyama inherits the theology of the cross from the theology of the pain of God, he avoids the weakness of its Christology. When he sets up

---

fundamentally stays away from Takizawa's "the primordial fact of Immanuel" when he necessitates the dialectics between immediate love and the wrath of God for the love rooted in the pain of God. For "if human sin does not enter into the world, the love of God loses the deepest ground of love. His theology [Kitamori's theology] assumes the logic that God requires human sin to sustain God's deepest love."

93. Sundermeier, *Das Kreuz als Befreiung*, 85–89. Regarding Kitamori's Christology, Sundermeier links Kitamori's weakness of Christology with the influence of Confucianism. The tsurasa originally in Japanese kabuki drama, the aesthetic principle to meet the pain of God, is heavily influenced by Confucianism. Confucianism is a tremendous system of ethics that prescribes all human relationships. The basic structure of human relationships is rooted in the relationship between father and son. This principle is applied from the subordinate to the superior, in the case of kabuki drama, from the killed son of the hero to the hero as father letting his son be sacrificed, and from the hero as a vassal to his lord respectively. As the drama concerns only the father's feeling of "tsurasa," Kitamori is also concerned about the pain of the Father, not the feeling of the Son, who was actually crucified and suffered on the cross of Jesus. He criticizes Kitamori for failing to take into consideration the suffering and death of Jesus of Nazareth. By the same token, he fails to make a Christology that has solidarity with victims.

the "broken Christ" as a theological criterion, he is willing to consider Asian massive suffering in the light of the crucified Christ.

CONCLUSION

I discussed that Kitamori develops his theology of the pain of God in a Japanese context. I have specified the concrete context of this "Japan." Piryns argues that the main question of the third generation of Protestant theologians in Japan is: "Is there a theology possible that is simultaneously *Japanese, orthodox,* and *contemporary*?"[94] Kitamori shares the main question at that period. He apologetically clarifies "what the Christian God is" from the theology of the cross. God is all embracing, but the continuity includes discontinuity between God's pain and human suffering. Therefore, the gospel cannot be synonymous only with love of God, but rather with the tertiary through the dialectics between love and wrath. Although current contextual theologians barely mention it, his view of God is inextricably connected with the reality of the human incapability of loving others as others. Kitamori's reason for rejecting immediate love lies in his perception of the reality: "we feel pain only when a loved one suffers or dies."[95] However, in saying that God loves us, he reminds us of the passage that says, "While we were enemies, we were reconciled to God" (Rom 5:10). God experiences the pain of the death of the Son. It is one dimension of the pain of the Father. The other side is the love of God who cannot deserve being loved. This is his contextual understanding of Luther's theology of the cross.[96]

When this main concern of Kitamori is developed into the Trinity, he mentions the essence of God as pain. God is the absolute other for us. Accordingly, immediate love without pain or discontinuity erupts when we analogically think of the love of God in line with natural and immediate love. His theology accepts otherness in his theological parameter. Nevertheless, just as other Asian theologies of the cross make the criticism that Kitamori does not come to the embodiment of suffering in his theology, the result is not only that he withdraws from the massive suffer-

---

94. Piryns, "Japanese Theology and Inculturation," 541.

95. Kitamori, *Theology of the Pain*, 53.

96. I recognize the common motif between Kitamori and Luther, when Luther summarizes the love of the cross: "Sinners are attractive because they are loved; they are not loved because they are attractive. For this reason, the love of man avoids sinners and evil persons," in Luther, "Heidelberg Disputation," 57.

ing of people but also that he fails to develop the "solidarity Christology." Moreover, Chung points out that it also results in Kitamori's failing to address the Asian-Buddhism tradition of Cosmic *dukkha,* which is the most precious "fusion of horizons" between Luther's theology of the cross and Buddhism, because of the deficiency of the embodiment of suffering in the cross.

Although I will return to crucial arguments in chapter 5, it is sufficient to say that Kitamori's theology of the cross cannot be connected with either the "solidarity Christology" or with the cosmic Christology. The former is crucial for liberation theology within and out of Asia, as I have explained. The latter is indispensable for a theology in Asia to encounter Asian "thickness" of religions and cultures more deeply than ever, because the cosmic Christ can be a "fusion of horizons" between Christian spirituality of the cross and Buddhist spirituality of cosmic dukkha. While Kitamori recognizes that "Buddhism is our tradition," he is often criticized by those who are willing to dialogue with Buddhism. Actually, the inter-faith dialogue between Christianity and Buddhism has proceeded outside of Kitamori's theology. I will explore the other line in which they understand the cross in the eyes of Buddhism in the following chapters. This is important to see Asian theology in a broad context of its religious-cultural diversity.

3

Buddhism and Theology of the Cross

INTRODUCTION

The Perspective of the Following Two Chapters

I WILL EXPLORE A theology of the cross in the Buddhist context in chapters 3 and 4. When a theology of the cross encounters the Asian religious matrix, a totally different tradition and culture come to us. When Wesley Ariarajah proposes intercultural hermeneutics in the Asian theological context, he argues that it is not a theological option but a critical necessity to make sense of the world.[1] Thinking of the Western setting for interfaith dialogue, it is not difficult to assume that a religious background is correspondent with its cultural tradition. There it is often presupposed that Christianity is anchored in the Western intellectual or cultural matrix, while other religions are in foreign cultures and traditions. However, when doing interfaith dialogue in Asia, this is not necessarily the case. Just as I will explore Yagi in regard to this remark, doing theology in Asia comes from more complicated reality of religions and cultures. Ariarajah signifies this complexity when he mentions "double belonging":

> There is not only greater knowledge and understanding of one another's religious traditions, but even the willingness to cross boundaries, leading to what has been called "double belonging," where a person rooted in a religious tradition adopts another tradition as an additional "spiritual home."[2]

1. Ariarajah, "Intercultural Hermeneutics," 92.
2. Ibid., 95.

The main reason for the double belonging lies in the fact that it does not work in Asia to divide a religion from other religions nor a religion from its cultural matrix. Therefore, the interfaith dialogue in Asia necessitates an *inter*-contextual perspective.[3] He presents three principles for practicing "inter-cultural hermeneutics" in an Asian context. First, it is not the same as comparative study of religion. Second, Asian theology cannot separate the intercultural from the inter-religious. Finally, intercultural hermeneutics arises out of experience, out of the need to make sense of an inter-religious reality, and out of the struggle to find meaning in the midst of and with the help of religious-cultural realities.[4] These elements require carefully listening to the voice of each religion, which should be connected to the others.

The complicated entity of religious cultures caused Xavier to have difficulty in translating the name of God and Kitamori to address the sharp distinction between immediate love and mediated love. Taking these elements into account, it is not necessarily possible to set up a clear division between Christianity and Buddhism or between West and East. In this sense, I keep in mind the words of Kim Kyoung-Jae that "culture is not like clothing that the human community simply puts on, but like the flesh, blood and soul of the shaping of the community."[5] The intercontextual perspective is a necessary approach to the web of Asian religious and cultural diversity and at the same time, to deal with what is different as being different in this context. Thus, when Fritsch-Oppermann says that Yagi is a "Christian existence in a Buddhism context," she points to the double warning for doing theology[6]—"Don't separate, but don't assimilate." For this an intercontextual reading of the cross is necessary.

I will first analyze the dialogue between Japanese Buddhism scholar Abe Masao and Western theologians. Interfaith dialogue is not the primary concern of my thesis, but it prepares me to move toward

---

3. In terms of the uses of *inter-, cross-,* and *trans-*, I rely on Schreiter's intercultural theology. In my understanding, *inter-* focuses on the interactive process of communication across cultural boundaries, while *trans-* and *cross-* are directed to emphasize generalizations based on the inter-cultural communication. See Schreiter, *New Catholicity*, 28–30.

4. Like Ariarajah, Kim Kyoung-Jae also recognizes the same point, and proposes the "fusion of horizon" in East Asian religious diversity, instead of the usage of syncretism. Kim, "Christianity and Culture," 147–63.

5. Ibid., 149.

6. Fritsch-Oppermann, "Christian Existence," 215–39.

the theology of Yagi Seiichi in the next chapter. I will find crucial topics for intercontextual reading of the cross in the following sections through exploring the interfaith dialogue between Christianity and Buddhism. Yagi shows the complexity of the combination of religious forms in both religions. Like Abe Masao, Yagi is one of the pioneers to open a dialogue between Buddhism and Christianity. Although Abe is Buddhist and Yagi is Christian, they share Buddhism's tradition in Japan, especially Zen Buddhism. Through exploring Yagi's theology, I will seek a way in which a theology of the cross encounters the Buddhist religious-cultural context.

Abe's Profile

Abe Masao was born in Osaka in 1915. He first sought a solution to his internal agony in the Pure Land School of Buddhism at a young age. While he studied Western philosophy at Kyoto Imperial University, he encountered Zen Buddhism through Hisamatsu Shinichi, one of the representative Zen masters and scholars of the Kyoto School. He gradually changed his Buddhist commitment from the Pure Land School of Buddhism to Zen Buddhism. Although Zen, through Hisamatsu, helped him to deepen his understanding of faith in Amida, he finally came to realize that even faith in Amida is a "sacred fiction" through awakening to absolute Nothingness.[7] This experience of conversion from faith in Amida to awakening to absolute Nothingness enabled him to propose a common ground of absolute Nothingness that makes it possible to go beyond Nietzschean nihilism, which he calls "relative nothingness." Accordingly, for Abe, interfaith dialogue is not merely for mutual understanding of different religions but is aimed at overcoming the secular anti-religious thought in the West and the East. It was after 1980, after his retirement as a professor of Western philosophy at Nara Education University, that he moved to the United States and started the full-dressed interfaith dialogue in the English-speaking world. Consider the following supplemental information about him to understand his position well.

First, as mentioned previously, he started his faith commitment in Pure Land Shin Buddhism (*Jyodo Shinshu*) and later converted to awakening to absolute Nothingness through Zen Buddhism. It is important to interfaith dialogue to take into account that he transferred his religious

---

7. Ives, *Divine Emptiness*, xv.

conviction from faith in Amida into awakening to Sunyata (emptiness). While he experienced the two kinds of religious experiences within Buddhist tradition, Yagi came to suggest these types of religious experiences within Christianity.

Second, as some theologians mention, it is necessary to remember that Abe's Buddhism belongs to Japanese Buddhism, and it does not represent all Buddhism. This is not meant to decrease the dignity of his Buddhist scholarship. However, when I survey the diversity of Asian religiosity in terms of the intercontextual reading of the cross, I come to other dimensions of Buddhism in a broader context. Japanese Buddhism shows a unique development, but at the same time, it is only one aspect of a broader Buddhism. When I explore the cosmic Christology of Paul Chung, I will return to this point.

Finally, his Buddhist scholarship, which cannot be separated from his religious conviction, was nurtured by the Kyoto School. The Kyoto School is a philosophical movement in which the founder, Kitaro Nishida, sought a creative dialogue between the Western philosophical tradition and Eastern, Japanese Buddhist tradition, in particular its philosophical tradition. Abe was mentored by Tanabe Hajime, a Buddhist philosopher who sought Buddhist Hegelianism and later was deeply influenced by Hisamatsu Shinichi, a Zen master. Accordingly, his tendency is more academic than empirical in terms of other Buddhist customs in Japan. Their philosophical reflection has been studied by postmodern philosophy today.[8] This Buddhism is critical of Christian theism. It makes Abe mention the *kenosis* of God. On the other hand, the Western theologians are critical of Abe's understanding of history and ethics. These topics are central for a theology of the cross in the Asian context.

BUDDHISM AND LIBERATION THEOLOGY

The Location of Argument

When Paul Knitter holds a dialogue with Abe Masao, he proposes two parallel sentences to clarify different perspectives between Buddhism and Christian liberation theology: "You cannot change the world unless you sit" and "You cannot sit unless you change the world." The fundamental question that Knitter brings into Buddhism, and to Abe's Zen

---

8. See Tracy, *Dialogue with the Other*.

Buddhism in particular, is about a theological epistemology in both religions. Knitter thinks that his question, "How to combine 'contemplation and action,'" can be deepened by learning from Buddhism.[9]

Zen encourages sitting until *Ku-zuru* (emptying oneself). It is a practice to liberate the practitioner from his or her own thoughts, speculation, words, and mind. Once one arrives at emptying, one is given the sight of everything on the basis of enlightenment to emptiness. Zen teaches that everyone lives his or her own transient life in a transitory world. Despite this transience, we try to ground ourselves in our own transience. It is the basic dilemma of the human condition. We even try to divide ourselves into each other in an errant recognition grounded on dualism. Zen refuses the distinctiveness of all sentient beings at the first level. Nobody establishes his or her own distinctiveness on the basis of transitoriness. Once we empty ourselves into emptiness, as much as we lose any distinctiveness, we are awakened to *Sunyata* (emptiness), from and to which all sentient beings come and go. Regarding subjectivity, that is the formless Self. From the enlightenment for emptiness one comes to perceive the distinctiveness of one's own self, which is co-originating and interdependent. This distinctiveness is different from the former one before awakening. This is distinctiveness based on indistinctiveness. This is the logic of a double negation: not two, not one. The practice converges in how to overcome dualism and ground one's life in the awakening to *Sunyata* (emptiness). Therefore, the question about social transformation that Knitter brings to him is hinged on this awakening.

On the other hand, Knitter presents the epistemology of liberation theology: the epistemological priority of the poor. We cannot know truth without taking right action, and vice versa: "The liberation claim is that we do not really know God or the Ultimate unless we are working for justice—that it is in the very experience of acting with and for the oppressed that God can be discovered in new and necessary ways today."[10] In a word, what liberation theology found is that "*action* has a certain *epistemological priority* over prayer or meditation or the explicitly religious."[11] In addition to this epistemology of orthopraxis, it is important in comparison with Abe that Knitter claims that doing justice should occur before we know and after we know. Because the "spirit lives within us before we confess

---

9. Abe and Knitter, "Spirituality and Liberation."
10. Ibid., 226.
11. Ibid., 235.

the Lord Jesus," through living and acting for justice, we come to know something new about God, the world, and history.

Abe's Response to Knitter

Abe presents a statement of his principles to understand his own thought in response to Knitter's comment:

> Each human being is a single existence who encompasses both horizontal and vertical dimensions. The horizontal dimension indicates the dimension of space and time, world and history, whereas the vertical dimension signifies the trans-spatial and trans-temporal dimension, namely the dimension of Self or God, that is religion. What I call practical condition, occasion or situation indicates the horizontal dimension, whereas what I call ground or source refers to the vertical dimension. . . . the horizontal dimension (spatio-temporal condition) and the vertical dimension (trans-spatio-temporal ground) are neither one nor two, and yet both one and two. . . . Unless we start from this dynamism, we cannot solve the problem of how to combine "meditation and action," "spirituality and liberation," and the problem of which has a priority, enlightenment or practice, action or prayer.[12]

The formula that Takizawa Katsumi presents is helpful here to understand Abe's anthropology. The formula of "inseparable, non identical, and irreversible" is applied to anthropology. A human being is composed of horizontal and vertical dimensions. These relationships should not be separated from one human existence (inseparable) but also should not be identified (non-identical) with it. Then, the vertical (religious) dimension, the dimension of awakening to emptiness, is ground, and the horizontal (spatio-temporal) is conditional. The former has priority over the latter. This relationship is irreversible. What is at stake in Abe's response is the irreversibility between the vertical and the horizontal.

Abe strictly prioritizes enlightenment (wisdom) over action (compassion). He argues that not until one is awakened to Sunyata can one rightly work for others because the enlightenment is ground (vertical), but action is condition (horizon). He is suspicious about whether Knitter considers action as ground for enlightenment or as condition. Even sitting cannot be an ultimate means for enlightenment in Zen.

---

12. Ibid., 242–3.

Rather, the Zen tradition is wary of absolutizing one method to come to enlightenment. Therefore, although sitting is generally understood as physically sitting, it is not essential. Walking, working, and sitting can be equally Zen practices. The most important thing for Zen practice is to accomplish and sustain "the well-composed, quiet mind under any circumstances."[13] From this methodological principle, Abe is suspicious that Knitter's liberation epistemology, orthopraxis, is in danger of absolutizing a way for enlightenment.

Their dialogue ends up as a simple exchanging of each religious position rather than being transformative and eventually reveals a fundamental difference in their perspectives. For Abe, the ultimate thing is whether one comes to enlightenment or not (gnosis). It is most crucial to seek an awakening formless Self/groundless ground as common ground between Christianity and Buddhism. However, Knitter, as a Christian, has a different perspective: "Christian life and identity are first of all a matter of *agape*—of living God's life, of loving, or doing what God does."[14] Therefore, Knitter can say this sentence, which is really problematic to Abe: "We do before we know. The spirit lives within us before we confess the Lord Jesus."[15] Knowing is not the primary thing here. The primary concern is to live with the God of love and justice. In other words, even if one does not know what one does, it is possible to say that one lives with God, works with the God of justice, and lives with the God of love. Knitter's epistemology is aimed at living *for* and *with* justice. The fundamental thing is to trust God, who works in the world for justice. This is Knitter's fundamental conviction by which liberation theology empowers people to commit to action for justice.

Both Buddhism and Christianity share the "core-experience of liberation," which Aloysius Pieris calls it.[16] However, the dialogue between Abe and Knitter represents the "polar experience" between Buddhism and Christianity: Christian *agape* and Buddhist *gnosis*. As far as I observe in the dialogue between Abe and Knitter, the polar experience remains polar. How can we continue to be in dialogue with Buddhism on this matter? What does Buddhism teach Christianity about the cross? They are different religions, but through dialogue, Abe and others seek

13. Ibid., 237.
14. Ibid., 235.
15. Ibid.
16. Pieris, "The Buddha and the Christ," 162.

common ground between Christianity and Buddhism. The dialogue that Abe practices shows the possibility to think about a theology of the cross in the Asian context. It makes it possible to put the suffering, kenosis of God, and ethics into its agenda.

BUDDHIST PERSPECTIVE FOR A THEOLOGY OF THE CROSS

Three North American theologians of the cross I surveyed in chapter 1 took a theology of *tentatio* most seriously in reconstructing Luther's theology of the cross in the context of the current reality of suffering. Regarding Bevans' typology, they explore Luther from the perspective of a "praxis model"; that is, knowing something cannot happen apart from one's own living context. The theological insight into suffering made a theologian of the cross resist the "technology of grace" and rethink the nature of God in the suffering world. The God who meets them in the abyss of the world is the crucified God. God suffered and died on the cross. This God is the resurrected Lord of the crucified. From there, they also see the different relationship of the crucified Christ with the world, history, and even nature. Buddhism is a sophisticated enough philosophy to take these elements seriously within its tradition but in a different way from the Christian tradition. A crucial difference appears to be the understanding of suffering.

Suffering in Buddhism

From the beginning, Buddhism is also a religion aiming at emancipation from suffering. However, suffering is understood as the consequence of ignorance about human potentiality for *nirvana*. Abe argues that there is Suffering (capital S) in and beyond concrete suffering in a phenomenal world.[17] The suffering that Buddhism perceives lies in both sufferings and pleasures, whether a human being is conscious or not of the fact, because Suffering is rooted in the fact that human life is bound to *samsara*, the cycle of birth and death. It comes from ignorance of transience. The

17. Abe, "Suffering," 74. He introduces an interesting episode that happened in his first lecture on Buddhism in the United States in 1966. When Abe told students how Gautama emphasized suffering in human life, one student commented that the reason for the emphasis resulted in the poverty of the age of Buddha. He said that Buddhism was irrelevant to contemporary Americans, because they were full of pleasure. To distinguish such a dualistic understanding, he proposes Suffering (capital S).

ignorance of transience brings about craving. Craving makes human beings attached to pleasure and suffering in a dualistic way. A human being is entangled in the duality of pleasure and suffering. The agent entangled with them is the ego. The ego strives to liberate the subject from suffering, but it ends up failing, because the agency itself is the cause of suffering. In this regard, Abe offers an impressive thought: "It is not that I *have* a dilemma, but that I *am* a dilemma."[18] When Buddhism seeks liberation from *Suffering*, it does not matter whether one is full of joy or sadness. Beyond both conditions, Suffering comes down to everyone.

The way of emancipation from Suffering relies on an awakening: enlightenment (*nirvana* or *satori*). This special knowledge through *nirvana* is not an objective knowledge that the subject consciously makes known. Rather, it is a kind of orthopraxis that keeps truth away from any cognitive-epistemological sequence. It is an awakening to *Sunyata* (emptiness or absolute nothingness). It is the groundless ground of all sentient beings. In the case of awakening to self, it is also called the true self or the Formless Self. Therefore, liberation from Suffering is knowing or awakening to the ground of self. This special way of knowing is full of paradox. The true Self is a formless self: no self. The more we try to know something like the true Self, the more we come to egolessness. That is why the ground in the Buddhist sense is nothing, emptiness, and groundlessness. Focusing on human liberation in terms of awakening to *Sunyata*, we can say that in order to live, we have to die: "to enter nirvana is not to die one's physical death, but to die the death of the ego and thereby to live a new Life, to live the life of the true Self."[19] It is called Great Death and Great Life.

However, the nothingness is not one-sidedly negative. Rather, it provides the ground of individual distinctiveness from the standpoint of emptiness. Abe says, "The universal and particular things are paradoxically one in the realization of Emptiness, which goes beyond the understanding which sees all things as reducible to the one."[20] To come to enlightenment or to emptiness/egolessness, two things are conditioned. One is that emptiness goes not only beyond dualism, by which the ego identifies who I am, but also beyond monism, which is a counter-concept against dualism or pluralism. This is neither monistic nor dualis-

---

18. Abe, *Zen and Western Thought*, 201.
19. Abe, "Suffering," 76.
20. Ibid., 77.

tic. That is why Buddhism does not have any theistic view in the end. God is not a substantial existence but an emptying God. This is the logic of double negation. Once one achieves double negation, one comes to double affirmation. It is the second point to come to enlightenment. Abe explains it like this: "Difference as it is, is sameness; sameness (of things in their suchness) as it is, is difference."[21] This is the source of wisdom and compassion. Buddhism does not take one substantial-independent being like the human ego and one transcendental God. Rather, the assumption of an independent distinction is the main cause of suffering. *Sunyata* brings about an insight of "dependent co-origination." Nothing (even God) can be independent of other sentient beings. Even God as a transcendental being must be emptied, because transcendence is the cause of dualism.

While Christian salvation is framed by the *I-thou* relationship in personal language, Buddhist liberation is featured by a cosmological awareness of absolute Nothingness. God, human beings, and nature, all sentient beings, are co-originated into each other, share the same nothingness, come from nothingness, and at the same time and because of this, all are different. Apart from the Christian tradition, in which the main topic of salvation is from sin as rebellion against God, Buddhism concentrates on the emancipation from the cosmological bondage to the cycle of life and death. Once one is awakened to the attachment to the transitory nature of the world, one comes to *nirvana* (enlightenment) to the true Self. Abe calls it "cosmo-existentialism or cosmo-personalism."[22]

When Buddhism addresses Suffering, it takes it into consideration that human beings are conditioned by the transitoriness of the cosmological cycle. Ignorance of cosmological bondage is entangled with any human activity, whether sufferings or pleasures. Once awakened to this bondage and transience, one can be free from them. They live with Great Life through Great Death. I am not I because I am egoless, and yet I am absolutely I because I am my true self, because I am my true Self. This awakening/enlightenment is the source of wisdom and compassion. Otherwise, any human activity, including acting for justice, becomes prey for absolutism or bottomless relativism. Suffering is aimed at this cosmic condition, including all sentient beings. This teaching of

21. Ibid., 77.
22. Ibid., 81.

Suffering enables Abe to engage in dialogue in terms of theologians who are engaged in current theologies of the cross.

Kenosis of Christ soku Kenosis of God

Taking Abe's notion of Suffering in terms of cosmic bondage, absolute Nothing is opened to the dependent and co-originating relationality of all sentient beings. To think of an independently substantial being like God is the consequence of human ignorance and craving for distinctiveness without enlightenment. Abe considers Philippians 2:5–8 as a most fascinating passage for the dialogue with Christianity. He thinks that the kenosis of Christ is compatible with *Sunyata* (emptying). Abe assures us that *Sunyata* is the ultimate reality for Buddhism; it is neither Being nor God. It is "absolute Nothingness" that drives the logic of double negation and comes to a paradoxical identity between transcendence and immanence. It rejects even that Sunyata remains Sunyata. The radical rejection of any objective perception should be applied to Sunyata itself. Abe contends that "emptiness not only empties everything else but also empties itself. Sunyata should not be conceived of somewhere outside one's self-existence, nor somewhere inside one's self-existence.... That is to say, the pure activity of absolute emptying is true Sunyata."[23] Abe's discussion is anchored in his own experience of Sunyata. There is no place beyond his own experience, but at the same time, his experience is the experience of Sunyata. Sunyata is beyond his experience of awakening to Sunyata. Therefore, Sunyata and self are dynamically and paradoxically identical in Zen Buddhism. This primacy of Sunyata enables Abe to approach the Christian God, and even allows him to give an interpretation of a biblical passage.

Abe seeks a common ground between Buddhism and Christianity in terms of the kenosis of Christ. It is a contrasting position with a way of seeking Christian identity in the transcendent God. Abe argues that, despite the fact that the passage of the kenosis of Christ comes close to the truth of Sunyata, Christianity tries to soften the impact of truth, because he understands Christ's kenosis as a transformation not only in appearance but also in substance. His understanding of kenosis implies a radical and total self-negation of the Son of God. Self-sacrificing love is the sign of the Son of God. Because of this sign, the Son of God to-

---

23. Abe, "Kenotic God," 27.

tally incarnated himself into humanity. Therefore, he is not the Son of God. Because he is not the Son of God due to his total kenosis, he is the Son of God.[24] He literally died on the cross. Because of his death, he is really Christ. We come to the affirmation of Christ through the negation. From the idea of "absolute nothingness," Abe's theology of the cross interprets "God is dead, not yet dead." Only if Christianity understands the death of Jesus as the Son of God are we led to Great Life, in which everything is dependent-co-originating, because "in and through total self-emptying . . . God *is* each and every thing."[25] Therefore, he advocates that the "kenotic God is the ground of the kenotic Christ."[26] The event of the self-emptying Son of God signifies the self-emptying of the Father up to absolute nothingness.

While Abe finds a compatible notion of absolute Nothingness in Karl Rahner's incarnation theology, he criticizes Rahner when he still says: "God can become something. . . . He possesses the possibility of *establishing* the other as his own reality by dispossessing *himself*, by giving himself way."[27] For Abe, this sentence shows the shortcoming of the kenosis of God because "become something" entails something like "traces of dualism." If God is totally love in terms of a self-emptying God, God must be totally untraceable by any conceptualization and objectification. Just as the Son becomes the Son because of the total nothingness of sonship, God must be total nothingness of divinity in order for each and every thing to be filled with God. This notion of the kenosis of God/Christ leads to the criticism that Abe eliminates the uniqueness of Jesus Christ because the absolute emptiness of God for each and every thing seems to exclude the statement that Jesus Christ alone is the incarnation of the Son of God in history.

Actually, Abe does not understand the kenosis of Christ in the sense of incarnation, by which the Son of God participates in the history of human beings. Rather, he recognizes the kenosis of Christ as "nothing but the revelation of this completely self-emptying Son of God through total

---

24. Ibid., 12. His formula is: 1) The Son of God is not the Son of God; precisely because he is not the Son of God, he is truly the Son of God; 2) Self is not self; precisely because it is not, self is truly self.

25. Ibid., 16.

26. Ibid., 16.

27. Ibid., 15.

abnegation of his divinity" as the sign of the all-loving God.[28] Therefore, as well as the self-emptying of the Son, the self-emptying of God can be affirmed for the divine incarnation in "each and every thing in the universe" by Abe. It should not be limited to Jesus Christ. Otherwise, he suspects that Christianity will continue to absolutize the historical point of Jesus of Nazareth, to the degree of excluding other possibilities of revelation in history. Every event in time and space and every human life and death are conditional but are opened to Sunyata.

Abe's basic stance is not necessarily anti-Christian. Rather, Abe tries to find a common ground between Buddhist absolute Nothingness and the Christian kenosis of Christ through his Buddhist interpretation of the kenosis of Christ. Altizer argues that a fundamental problem of Christian identity in the modern age lies in the fact that the "objective identity of transcendent transcendence"[29] has been crushed. He positively states that Buddhism at the Kyoto School presents the "paradoxical identity of the transcendence and the immanence of God," and makes it possible for Buddhism to be "Buddhist and modern at once."[30] In comparison with the total kenosis of God, Altizer suggests that the crucifixion of God can be a common ground between Christianity and Buddhism:

> Transcendence disappears in Buddhist thinking, and it is just such thinking that can now apprehend the kenosis of Godhead itself, and a kenosis that is the source and ground of an absolute presence of the Godhead in the absolute absence or death of God. Abe, Nishitani, and Nishida can know the death of God in the Incarnation itself, and thereby know the death of God as the compassion of God, a compassion that is the very embodiment of the absolute emptying of the Godhead. That very emptying is the fullness of Godhead itself, a fullness which is emptiness, and a fullness that is the emptiness of self-negation of God. Can such an emptiness or self-negation be present or manifest upon a historical horizon determined by the transcendence of transcendence. . . . each would be open to a wholly immanent transcendence, an immanent transcendence that Buddhism can know as the absolute's own subjectivity.[31]

28. Ibid., 18.
29. Altizer, "Buddhist Emptiness," 70.
30. Ibid., 71.
31. Ibid., 72.

Jürgen Moltmann also affirms Abe's emptying God. Moltmann understands that Abe's perspective is not just a dialogue between Buddhism and Christianity but a kind of praxis to seek a way in which both religions can work together against contemporary anti-religious forces.[32] When Moltmann mentions the "monotheism of modern Western religions," he appreciates the fact that Abe illuminates a different picture of Christian identity by focusing on the kenosis of Christ in Philippians 2.[33] He also agrees that the kenosis of Christ is grounded on divine unselfish love. However, he disagrees with Abe in that he radicalizes the substantial God into absolute nothingness ("great zero"). It is not because Moltmann claims "transcendent transcendence" but because he attempts to establish Christian identity about God in a different way from either Tellutrian substantial oneness or Abe's absolute Nothingness. While Abe identifies the Christian God in Christianity's metaphysical and monotheistic tradition and presents an alternative by emptying God, Moltmann rather identifies God as "community": "The unselfishness in the eternal love and unity of the Trinitarian God is *perichoresis*: community in mutual interdependence and interpenetration."[34] Although Moltmann affirms with Abe that "the divinity of the Trinitarian God is kenosis," he maintains the distinction between person and nature within the Trinity. Instead of radical immanent transcendence, he comes to a doxology for the Trinitarian mystery of love. On this point, he develops a "perichoretical network of reciprocal sympathy."[35] I will explore the development of this perichoretical theology in chapter 5.

Unlike Altizer and Moltmann, Hans Küng and Wolfhart Pannenberg present a common critique of Abe's kenosis of God, maintaining Christian monotheistic identity. Both suggest that the biblical passage does not support that God the Father, not the Son of God, is the emptying God. Küng even questions the primacy of Sunyata for broader Buddhist schools.[36] David Chappell also raises the fact that Zen Buddhism was defeated in Tibetan tradition in the eighth century in the debate about the primacy between enlightenment and compassion.[37] On

32. Shore, "Abe Masao's Legacy," 302.
33. Moltmann, "God is Unselfish Love," 118.
34. Ibid., 119–20.
35. Ibid., 121.
36. Küng, "God's Self-Renunciation," 207–23.
37. Chappell, Introduction to *Divine Emptiness*, 16.

the other hand, Chappell argues a more important point about Abe and his understanding of Emptiness: "Abe engages in dialogue based on his own religious experience, not primarily on an inherited set of dogmatic or institutionalized positions."[38] His experience is rooted in Hisamatsu Zen, which emphasizes the realization of emptiness within the ego-self.[39] Heinrich Ott deepens the dialogue in line with Abe's experiential dimension, not a dogmatic dimension.[40] However, overall, many interlocutors question Buddhism's Sunyata and ethics through the dialogue with Abe. This is another topic in their dialogue.

History and Ethics

Buddhist awakening to Sunyata, the groundless ground, is wary of any kind of absolutism in time and space, even in terms of Christ and God in Christianity. However important Jesus is to Christianity, it cannot be the ground for everything and everyone but can be *kien* (opportunity) for enlightenment rather than *konkyo* (ground). Abe's claim functions in a deconstructive way. This tendency brings about the issue of history and ethics.

According to Abe, Buddhist understanding of time is entirely without beginning and without end. Therefore, time is also reversible in the light of enlightenment or an awakening (*nirvarna*) because "time moves from moment to moment, each moment embracing the whole process of time."[41] From this realization of *samsara*, the beginningless and endless reality of living-dying, wisdom and compassion are operating to emancipate innumerable sentient beings from transmigration.[42] What is at stake is how to realize the awakening to "this moment" in the midst of living-dying process. The reversibility that Abe mentions is the reversibility of historical meaning through enlightenment. Time is not equal to history: "Time becomes 'history' when the factor of spatiality (worldhood, *Weltlichkeit*) is added to it."[43] Abe recognizes that history retains a "repeatable uniqueness or once-and-for-all nature" but admits the prob-

38. Ibid., 14.
39. Ibid., 14–15.
40. Ott, "The Convergence," 127–35.
41. Abe, "Kenotic God," 59.
42. Ibid., 60.
43. Ibid., 60.

lem is that the notion of the reversibility of time is transferred into the reversibility of history.[44] When he argues that the history of Buddhism is the "history of vow and act," the tension between the reversibility of time and the unrepeatable uniqueness of history is dissolved into the "vertical dimension" of an awakening by inserting the dichotomy between vertical and horizontal. While Abe divides time and history, he also distinguishes two dimensions: "the aspect of continuity or forward movement and the aspect of discontinuity or 'trans-descending' movement."[45] In saying this, he argues that the "continuity of time without the realization of its discontinuity is an abstraction."[46] This is right. However, again, he dissolves the "horizontal dimension" and the "irreversibility of the historical event" into the "reversibility of time." Then, the irreversibility of the historical event that Keller mentions in her first response to Abe's presentation is replaced with the possibility to "alter the meaning of our past deed."[47]

Catherine Keller is one who has willingly taken Buddhist elements into her feminist theology, as she finds incredible wisdom in the teachings like the "awakening to the nonsubstantiality and the interdependence of everything in the universe."[48] However, she criticizes Abe in that his way of using these teachings is deconstructive rather than constructive. She asserts three criticisms. First, she criticizes his tendency to reinforce the more patriarchal implications of the kenotic Christ in his identification of self-surrendering with love.[49] Second, regarding the self-emptying God (the kenosis of God is "each and every thing"), Abe tends to annihilate even God into oneness. Keller emphasizes the difference of all beings: "Because God is in everything, God is fully immanent. Because God is in everything, God is not identical with anything. Because God is in everything, God transcends anything. God is fully transcendent

---

44. Ibid., 60. Abe continues to say that "since time is understood to be entirely beginningless and endless and thus reversible, the unidirectionality of time and the uniqueness of each moment essential to the notion of history are not clearly expressed in Buddhism."

45. Abe, "A Rejoinder," 192.

46. Ibid., 192.

47. Ibid., 193.

48. Keller, "Scoop up the Water," 103.

49. Ibid., 104. See also Cobb, "On the Deepening of Buddhism" 94–96. Cobb also indicates that the teaching of inter-dependency and nonsubstantiality should be emphasized in a constructive way for ethics, not as a principle of negation.

because fully immanent."⁵⁰ She carefully distinguishes pantheism from panentheism. Finally, Keller configures the notion of the reversibility and irreversibility of time and history that I summarized above, but she disagrees with the one-sided irreversibility of history. Her point is that "transformation is not reversal."⁵¹

She agrees with Abe about the reversibility of history in terms of the meaning of past events, but the indispensable point is that it does not cancel out anything that happened in the past. She delivers her suspicious voice to Abe, "Abe's revision of Buddhism can finally valorize . . . the particularity of individuals, groups, and historical moments."⁵² Abe also affirms the reversibility of time, but it is at the level of vertical-religious dimension. But from her perspective of counter-hegemonic action, irreversibility is just as important as reversibility: there is no reversibility without irreversibility: "the struggle to remember and confront the particular history of one's karmic bondage is the only way to free oneself of it, to discard the past as illusion would yield only an illusory liberation."⁵³ Apart from the deconstructive strategy of Abe, Keller is willing to develop Buddhist teachings in a constructive way in order to insert the dependent and co-originating nature of all sentient beings into the "horizontal" moment: "I believe that they [ground and condition] need to be *con-fused*, that is, understood as 'fused horizons'(Gadamer), incapable of being conceived in separation from one another. Abe's facile oppositions of time and eternity . . . strike me more as symptomatic of ultra-Western dualisms seeking a Hegelian cure than as Buddhist."⁵⁴

While Abe tries to secure the "vertical" dimension of history by cutting off the horizontal-forward move of time, Keller attempts to insert the kenosis doctrine into this present moment, "so that we begin to discern the depth, complexity, and mystery of time itself, of fleshly life and its barely explored spiritual potentials."⁵⁵ Abe claims that there is no enlightenment without the horizontal dimension, but it's aimed not to preserve the irreversibility of the past event and to embody the "vertical" liberation in the "horizontal" liberation—social ethics. Rather, Abe

50. Ibid., 109.
51. Keller, "More on Feminism, Self-Sacrifice," 214.
52. Keller, "Scoop up the Water," 110.
53. Keller, "More on Feminism," 212.
54. Ibid., 215.
55. Ibid., 215.

contends that the socio-historical dimension is merely the place to find the "real" liberation on the basis of vertical-eternal liberation.[56]

CONCLUSION

In modern history, Christianity has not engaged in dialogue with Buddhism for a very long time. Abe is one of pioneers who open-mindedly entered into dialogue with Western theologians. Abe is familiar with Western philosophical and theological heritage and offered an opportunity for them to mutually understand each other. It is also worth noting that he attempts to touch on the point of contact with Christian faith in terms of the cross within the general climate of Buddhism's antipathy for a theology about the cross, its historical symbol of conquest, and arrogance. He provides a subsequent lead for the dialogue of Buddhist *Sunyata* with Christian *kenosis* in terms of the view of God. On the other hand, in this proposal of intercontextual reading of the cross, it is also crucial to reflect on the debate about history and ethics. Keller's criticism of Abe, which overlaps the critical point by Cobb and Moltmann, is indispensable to develop a theology of the cross in the Buddhist context. In saying "Buddhist context," I recognize myself in that. Thus, personally, I cannot hear this debate as merely a Christian theologian, but rather as the one who shares the Buddhist culture and tradition in my cultural background. What is common between Abe and Kitamori only in terms of history and ethics is that they clearly distinguish the historical (horizontal) Jesus from kerygmatic (vertical) Christ or God. Yes, I agree with the clear distinction. However, Keller's point is that their distinctions make the embodiment of the cross, and thus, the embodiment of suffering, evaporate from their discourses.

Despite Abe's insight into the cosmic dimension of Suffering, his discourse about the kenosis of God is eventually reduced into individual awakening in the universe (cosmoexistentialism). As Westhelle shows in his theology of the cross, the cross is the "thorn of history." This is also the history of use and abuse. What Thomsen, Solberg, and Westhelle all show is that the revelation of God is nothing outside of a particular place. Abe most likely agrees with this. However, the particular place of revelation does not mean that the particularity of time and history

---

56. Ibid., 198. Cf. Chung, "Dietrich Bonhoeffer," 127–46. Chung introduces the case of Thich Nhat Hanh as an example of a constructive way of co-originating.

is merely place (*topos*) to bring the awakening of absolute Nothing or something ultimate. Conversely, their theologies of the cross pay attention to a direction from divine activity to the "horizontal." We cannot perceive a divine thing without embodiment. Losing the mutual direction, Christian theology also comes to say that "horizontal liberation cannot realize liberation."

Therefore, a theology of the cross needs to grapple with the double direction between the "horizontal" and the "vertical." The crucifixion of Jesus retains the face of "eternity" but cannot be separated from the historical event. That is the function of Westhelle's third key: the "epistemic key." Abe's dichotomy between the horizontal and vertical is similar to a Christian logic of "ultimate" and "penultimate" in terms of the forgiveness of sin, as Thomsen tries to overcome it in dialogue with Forde. What is at stake for both Buddhism and Christianity is not to underestimate the irreversibility of particular history. A theology of the cross stimulates the memory of people who witnessed the crucifixion of Jesus, and by the same token, the eschatological vision of people in a "con-fused" manner between here and there. This crucified Jesus is the one who was resurrected. The reversibility of the cross event does not set off the irreversibility of the scar.

4

Theology without the Cross

OVERVIEW OF YAGI'S THEOLOGY

Profile of Yagi

YAGI IS THE ONE who opened the way for interfaith dialogue between Christianity and Buddhism. As the result of his reflection on his local cultural background, he proposes a new way of speaking about God, because he is not satisfied with both the ontological approach to God (Greek tradition) and the personified approach (I-Thou) in the Judeo-Christian tradition. In the place of these approaches, he proposes recognition of God as action. The recognition of action lies in the experience of awakening. This action of God is exchangeable with the work of Holy Spirit in Yagi's theology, the Buddhist context. He develops this line of thought in dialogue with Buddhism.

Yagi Seiichi was born in Yokohama, Japan, in 1932. He grew up in a Christian family during the war period, when Christianity had difficulty under the control of ultra-nationalism. His father was a follower of Uchimura Kanzo, the founder of the independent non-church movement (*mukyo-kai*) in Japan. After he graduated from Tokyo University, he studied at Göttingen University in Germany, where he studied the New Testament under the instruction of Joachim Jeremias, Ernst Käsemann, and others. However, after returning to Japan, the scholar who had the most influence on him was Takizawa Katsumi.[1] Yagi was

---

1. Takizawa was already well known among scholars in Japan as one of representative scholars of the Kyoto school. He learned theology from Karl Barth, and later, his formula of the distinction between the primary contact and the second contact prompted

a professor at the Tokyo Institute of Technology until his retirement. During that time and after his retirement, he was a guest professor at the International Christian University in Tokyo, at the University of Bern in Switzerland, from which he received an honorary doctorate, and at Hamburg University in Germany.

In the introduction to *The Structure of New Testament Thought*, Yagi introduces a personal experience that enabled him to grasp the key for understanding of Zen Buddhism.[2] This experience that he calls *immediate experience* (*chokusetsu keiken*) is crucial to understanding his theology. When he was in Germany, he visited his father's fiend, Wilhelm Gundert, who was a missionary to Japan and a translator of Zen texts into German. Gundert gave him an offprint of the German translation of the *Bi-Yan-Lu*, a classic Zen text, when he left:

> I read the text in the express train to Göttingen. Fortunately the train was empty; I could sit by myself in a corner and steep myself in reading undisturbed. I read it with such zeal and such concentration that finally I grew tired. Exhausted and relaxed, I looked at the country scene near Kässel; the rain had just stopped and the clouds were breaking up. The rift in the clouds expanded so that blue sky became visible. Then suddenly the saying flashed through my mind: "Open expanse—nothing holy." I got up and looked around. Something had happened to me which I could not immediately understand. All the things that I saw looked quite different from before, although they remained the same. The first words I said to myself were: "I took the tree for the tree. How wrong that was!" What I took to be a tree was in reality only the public concept "tree." I first introduced it into the "object" without being aware of it, and when I saw it, I expounded only what I had put into it beforehand, and I called only that "knowing an object." So I was simply recognizing again what I had already long known. But that was no seeing, no encounter with being. However, now I saw the "tree" as it originally showed itself, before the formation of any concept.[3]

---

him to criticize both Christianity, including his teacher, Barth, and Buddhism.

2. Seiichi, *Shinyaku Shisou*.

3. His Kässel experience has been introduced in several writings in Japanese, German, and English. I quote here from the English version in Küster, *Many Faces of Jesus Christ*, 96–97.

Although it was not until later that he came to realize what this experience meant, he explains that it was a kind of Zen experience, an awakening:

> It is a Zen experience. It is the same one as the "pure experience (immediate experience)" that Nishida Kitaro writes in *Study of Virtue (Zen no kenkyu)*. However, unlike Nishida, my experience is also a question about language. One of the aspects of Zen experience can be paraphrased as "that a human being that is the Self *soku* the ego awakes to the Self" or "the event that the Self shows itself *to* and *in* the ego."[4]

Triple Otherness

In light of the "immediate experience before linguistic expression is given," he has rethought God, the world, and being a human. He develops the encounter with the other into a triple dimension of otherness: 1) the subject-object immediate experience; 2) I-Thou immediate experience; 3) the ego-self immediate experience. The Kässel experience is classified into the first one, the subject-object immediate experience. In saying, "I took the tree for the tree. How wrong that was," it means nothing other than that he encountered the original nature of the tree, which broke through the network of language. The "tree" is no longer the tree that is represented. The simultaneous grasp of both the otherness and the original nature of "object," "Thou," and "self" is characteristic of Yagi's theology. It represents the paradoxical connection of otherness and original nature by the logic soku. Regarding the I-Thou immediate experience, he says that he received it when he made his faith confession of Christ's atoning death, though he came to this notion after he met Zen Buddhism.[5]

God is the one who speaks to human beings. The personal response between them brings the I-Thou immediate experience. However, in order to recognize this experience, the third *immediate experience* is required. The third one, the ego-self immediate experience, means the encounter with the other within subject. The other is the original subject and at the same time, the marginalized subject in the condition of non-awakening. An awakening primarily is to awake to this reality. However, unlike Zen, for Yagi, the original subject means Christ. Here,

4. Yagi, *Structure of New Testament Thought*, 31.
5. Ibid., 32–33.

the relationship between Christ and human beings is understood perichoretically. Yagi verifies the immediate experience through the study of the New Testament. When Yagi finds another form of language in Zen Buddhism, he starts to reread the Scripture in a different way. That is *field theory* theology.

Awakening soku Faith

Field theory theology makes it possible to talk about Christian faith from the perspective of an awakening. Yagi's latest writing, *The Structure of the New Testament Thought*, is an attempt to bridge the faith tradition with the awakening tradition in the New Testament. He proposes that the fundamental experience of the New Testament is "the experience of conversion from the mere ego to the ego awakened to the self."[6] Buddhist language appears to him not as an irrelevant other but as internalized otherness within his Christian faith. Abe critiques Wilfred Cantwell's article for proposing the faith-in form as a common religious form among world religions. He corrects it because Buddhism prioritizes an awakening form over the faith-in form.[7] However, more radically, Yagi contends that, like the faith-in form, the awakening-form has existed in the Christian tradition from the beginning, from the time of the New Testament. Both forms present the diversity of religious experience of early Christians in terms of Jesus's life, death, and resurrection. Using the Buddhist logic of soku, he argues that both the faith-in form and the awakening form should simultaneously occur: faith in Christ soku awakening to Christ. Christ is revealed to us as the resurrected other, but simultaneously, Christ is awakened within the subject as the other: other *soku* self; their relationship is not one, not two; inseparable, but non-identical.

---

6. Ibid., x.

7. Abe, "Faith and Self-Awakening," 12–24. In Buddhism, although Buddha as a person is important, his teaching itself rejects that his existence is central for others' salvation. Rather, it teaches to become "a realize of *Dhama*." The subject of awakening is not Gautama as a person but *Dhama*. Abe summarizes: "*Dharma* is the subject of its own self-awakening and you are a channel of its self-awakening."

Theology without the Cross 89

Linguistic Study

In order to clarify the awakening form in Christian faith, Yagi develops linguistic analysis of the language of theology, particularly of New Testament language.[8] His linguistic study of the New Testament shows that the language of the New Testament has two theological languages to reflect on God. The two language forms bring about two kinds of theology. The first is the *personification language* (*jinkaku-shugi-teki gengo*), which provides the frame of I-Thou for the description of salvation. This language form takes on the narrative form of salvation in the New Testament, representing the drama of salvation on the basis of invitation-response between God and human beings. Although it is not a unilateral drama, it has commonality with the fact that the center of the divine drama lies in Jesus Christ (his coming, death, resurrection, and epiphany). This personification language/theology comes from reflection upon the religious experience of the authors and their faith communities in the New Testament. This notion of Yagi's is compatible with Bultmann's idea that the New Testament is the record of "self-understanding" of the early church:

> I have most learned from Bultmann's writings in terms of New Testament study. His hermeneutics of de-mythologize is to take the *self-understanding* of the New Testament from the texts and tries to re-talk it in contemporary existentialist manner. Although the New Testament explains God, Christ and human salvation in an objective manner, it does not come from objective observation, but from the *objectification* of the self-understanding. This is basically right. The readers of this writing [Yagi's writing] will see that I paraphrase Bultmann's "self-understanding" into "self-awakening" and also I understand the language of the biblical texts not as "descriptive language," but as "representative (or aesthetic) language."[9]

Religious language, which is an expression of the religious understanding of a particular event, can be communicated according to whether communicators resonate in the light of the reader's own experience, not by whether its content is objective. The authors of the New Testament recorded their religious experience with Jesus Christ in a *descriptive* way (*kijyutu-teki*). However, although the form of the language is descrip-

---

8. The full development of his linguistic study is in *Shukyo to gengo*.
9. Yagi, *Structure of New Testament Thought*, 27.

tive, its religious expression is grounded in the "representative" (*hyogengengo*) language. The New Testament reports about Jesus Christ are not a historical-objective description in a modern sense. Yagi continues to argue that the personification language, which embodies a descriptive way, is in danger of absolutizing itself with dogmatic-objective claims if one understands it only through modern historical consciousness.

Another language form is field theory language. While personification language is primary in the New Testament, this language/theology is minor but indispensable for one to grasp the meaning of what the personification language expresses. This language form and its theology allow one to grasp the relationality of God-Christ-the Spirit with a human being:

> For instance, [the relationship is expressed as] "God is Christ and Christ in believers" or "believers in Christ and Christ in God." Christ appears in believers. Holy Spirit works in believers. Here, God, Christ and Holy Spirit are depicted as action, and thus neither person nor substance. It is typical in Paul's saying that "To me, to live is Christ (Phil. 1:21)." This writing calls this theology the "*field theory* theology (*bashoron-teki shingaku*)."[10]

Yagi finds the awakening form of religious experience, especially in the theology of John and in part of Paul's letters. God is understood as "action, agency or function (*sayo*)," and at the same time, "field or *topos* (*ba*)." He defines the field and action:

> The human beings live in God, and God lives in human beings. The basic category (in the *field theory* theology) is *action* and *field*. The basic content is the unity in the field of action (*sayo-itsu*). This theology comes from the self-experience of conversion of the way of life (conversion from the mere ego to the ego awakened to the self/Self). The place that this conversion occurs is the *field* of *action*.[11]

While personification theology expresses salvation in the form of calling-response between God and human beings, field theory theology takes the form that is perichoretic, like "A in B." This "in" is not ontological but relational or functional in Yagi's theology. Personification theology and field theory theology are not necessarily mutually exclusive. The

10. Ibid., viii.
11. Ibid., viii.

reason Yagi is sensitive to the use of language is because he knows about the risk of theology, as he says: "God can be personal and field-like, but God is neither person nor field. What we can speak is just the aspect of God's action as person or as *field theory*."[12] Nobody can depict God by observation. What we can do is to express the work or action of God that is directed to each of us.

These language forms are different expressions of common experience within the subject at the bottom of a personified form of faith. It is the "conversion of the mere ego into the ego awakened to the Self." This conversion is explained as God's action for salvation in the *personification* theology and is also depicted as the perichoretic relationship between God and human beings that occurs as a consequence of the conversion in field theory theology. When personification theology pervades without resonating with the experience of conversion, the description of the drama of salvation is in danger of falling into absolutism and exclusivism by objectification of the report of religious experiences in the New Testament. Yagi insists that the fundamental experience of conversion takes place in the bottom of religious experience to develop the personification theology in which Christian faith is enacted. They require each other in a complementary way. I will explore this notion in Yagi's explanation through the study of Paul's theology in the next section, which provides a juxtaposition between these theologies in terms of a theology of the cross.

THE PERSONIFICATION THEOLOGY SOKU THE FIELD THEORY THEOLOGY

Yagi's Typology of Personification Language

When Yagi finds the negative connection of personification language with the objectification of the experience of the New Testament's text, he attempts to de-personify it, just as Bultmann de-mythologized it. Personification theology represents two major theological modes. Because both theologies of salvation are relevant to understanding the cross of Jesus Christ, I will explore his argument here. Yagi recognizes four models of the structure of New Testament thought through his linguistic study. What the analysis of structure means is to first view the

---

12. Ibid., 209–10.

whole text of the New Testament from the viewpoint of the structure, though he emphasizes that the form of the gospel text is narrative, not the thematic thesis like Western philosophy or not an objective-historical report in a modern sense. Yagi thinks that the plot of the narrative decides the structure of thought and qualifies the rule of performance of each word and sentence. Like creating a Latin grammar from Cicero's writing, he attempts to construct the rule of performance from the text of the New Testament. Thus, his study of the New Testament moves from historical criticism to the study of structure.[13] The models of the narrative structure of religious thought/experience in the New Testament are listed below:

> Model 1: The *unmediated-restoration* model (*fukki-gata*) (e.g., Jesus's self-awakening to the reign of God).
>
> Model 2: The *self-liberating* model (*dasshutsu-gata*) (e.g., the gospel of Thomas).
>
> Model 3: The *mediated salvation* model (*kyujyo-gata*) (e.g., the kerygma that Jesus died for our sins).
>
> Model 4: The *mediated liberation* model (*kyushutsu-gata*) (e.g., the unity with Christ through his participation in our fate).

My purpose is not to explore the entire approach of his structural study. Rather, it is limited to his de-personified understanding of theology of the cross. He does this to avoid exclusivism and absolutism and to find a common ground between Christianity and Buddhism in terms of awakening to the Self/Christ. The main structure of the New Testament is narrative, and it functions to clarify the drama of salvation. The unmediated-restoration model (m. 1) and the self-liberating model (m. 2) are more simple and basic structures and provide grounds for the mediated salvation model (m. 3) and the mediated liberation model (m. 4). The unmediated-restoration model (m. 1) develops into the mediated salvation model (m. 3), and the self-liberating model (m. 2) develops

---

13. Ibid., 91. The difference from historical criticism becomes clear when he says: "Literal critics who take priority on historical criticism often argue that the analysis of structure is subjective because the structure is constructive apart from the intention of authors. However, such a criticism is likely to say that it is subjective and not trustful for linguistics to make Latin grammar from Cicero's writing. Is it right to say that one should not make Latin grammar by reason that Cicero did not write anything about Latin grammar? . . . 'Structure' is internalized in text."

Theology without the Cross 93

into the mediated liberation model (m. 4). These developments are just structural. They do not mean the successive development of contents.

The structure of the unmediated-restoration model (m. 1) is discovered in the texts that should be ascribed to be Jesus's own words. The thought of the unmediated-restoration model (m. 1) does not include a savior as mediator or helper. This model, the religious thought of Jesus, would be *structurally* developed into the mediated salvation model (m. 3). On the other hand, the self-liberating model (m. 2) cannot be found in the text of the New Testament, though Philippians 2:6–11 alludes to it. Rather, Yagi finds the text parallel to this model in the gospel of Thomas. The self-liberating model (m. 2) is also developed into the mediated liberation model (m. 4) *structurally*. The mediated salvation model (m. 3) describes the history of salvation.

The history of salvation is the drama of redemption of fallen humanity as played by God on the stage of the world. The death on the cross and resurrection of Jesus Christ take a core of the narrative of redemption as the atoning work of Christ in the framework of salvation history. On the other hand, the mediated liberation model (m. 4) is also the narrative of salvation, but unlike the history of salvation in the mediated salvation model (m. 3), its plot is that Christ was sent by God from heaven and liberated the human beings captivated by evil power through his own death and resurrection. Believers receive salvation by participation in Christ's death and life. Thus, the mediated salvation model (m. 3) and the mediated liberation model (m. 4) have been developed as soteriology through the cross-resurrection of Jesus Christ. The unmediated-restoration model (m. 1) and the self-liberating model (m. 2) remain basic structures that provide grounds for these models.

Classification of Models

There are two kinds of categories to distinguish each model. The first category is *by whom* salvation and is accomplished in each model (i.e., whether there is a mediator or not). The unmediated-restoration model (m. 1) and the self-liberating model (m. 2) do not need any mediator. In the case of the unmediated-restoration model (m. 1), the parable of the prodigal son in Luke that Jesus teaches is typical. When the prodigal son was down in misery, "He came to himself" (Luke 15:17). He returned (repented) by himself through self-awakening. The self-liberating model (m. 2), the Gnostic model, is a similar case. In the gospel of Thomas, the character in heaven goes down to this world to take up a pearl, which is the metaphor for human beings captivated in this world. However, he carelessly falls asleep there. Reminding himself of his heavenly robe, he wakes up and goes back to heaven. As well as the unmediated-restoration model (m. 1), the self-liberating model (m. 2) shows the structure of self-awakening by oneself. Therefore, they do not need any mediator toward salvation structurally. On the other hand, the mediated salvation model (m. 3) and the mediated liberation model (m. 4) necessitate the existence of mediator or savior to save human beings, whether savior by atonement or through participation in human fate. In other words, model 3 and model 4 structurally require Christology.

The other category is dependent on how each model grasps the condition of the world in which human beings recognize themselves as the ones who should be saved. Regarding this point, the unmediated-restoration model (m. 1) and the mediated salvation model (m. 3) recognize the condition where fallen human beings are located. Their humanity is damaged, but the place is not *minus*. The *minus* means that they are captive in something like evil power, in which divine power does not pervade. We often find in the synoptics the mention of the devil and evil powers in connection with Jesus. However, Jesus's teaching is basically convinced that anything and anyone is under the reign of God, no matter what our human realities. On the other hand, the self-liberating model (m. 2) and the mediated liberation model (m. 4) understand the human situation as being captive to evil powers apart from divine power. Therefore, the fallen level of human beings is *minus*.

The diversity of structures clarifies the different ways of understanding their experience of God through the Jesus event, which Yagi expands into the religious thought of Jesus himself: model 1. In our discussion, the mediated salvation model (m. 3) and the mediated liberation model (m. 4) are important because these narrative structures are correspondent with the two types of theologies of salvation through Jesus Christ: salvation by faith in Christ as the savior of sinners and salvation by faith in Christ who participates in human-captivated fate. What is at stake is to propose two types of salvation narratives that are structurally different. They cannot be compatible with each other. Nevertheless, they co-exist in the New Testament.

It is Paul's theology that presents both the mediated salvation model (m. 3) and the mediated liberation model (m. 4). All personification theologies have self-understandings of their religious experience at the base of their own theological descriptions. They express the experience of Jesus Christ as Savior in the language of personification. Thus, the New Testament, which is written in personification language, is not a historical and objective report but a description based on the self-understanding of the writers' experiences. At the level of the self-understanding of experience, Yagi finds common ground with Buddhism: awakening.

Only when one understands that the personification language is not objective reporting can personification theology be compatible with field theory theology, which is directly concerned with the relationship between God and the subject in terms of awakening. Although the personification models (m. 3 and m. 4) express their own understanding of the religious experiences in the form of *faith*, field theory theology does it in the form of awakening in Zen Buddhism. In other words, the awakening form of religious experience lies on the other side of the faith expression in the New Testament. This notion is a radical point that makes Yagi go beyond merely comparative study of religions. He finds awakening form in the faith form of model 4 in Paul and in the gospel of John. It is necessary to approach the text from the awakening form to the faith form.

He argues that we first have to start with the recognition that there are two different religious thoughts in Paul. Model 3 and model 4 are mixed up in Paul's thought.[14] These models, the mediated salvation model (m. 3) and the mediated liberation model (m. 4), are as one in their evangelical proclamation, "Believe in Christ, who died on the cross and was raised." Here we find the integration between both theologies. However, we cannot find integration within the content of each theology. Yagi argues that the mediated salvation model (m. 3) is the interpretation of the death of Jesus by the early Church. They believed that the cross of Jesus is atoning work. However, the Christ of model 4 is not the Savior who performed the atoning death for our sin. He is the Savior as a liberator from sin, death, and evil through his own overcoming of them. Believers can be saved by participation in his death and life.

Accordingly, the mediated liberation model (m. 4) shows the perichoretic experience between Paul (or believers) and Christ. Paul lives

---

14. See Schweitzer, *Mysticism of Paul*. Yagi recognizes Romans 3:23–26 as the representative passage that these models are mixed. Regarding the exegesis of this passage, Yagi refers to Käsemann, "Zum Verständnis von Röm. 3:24–26."

in Christ and Christ lives in Paul, though "in" here retains different nuances. That is, he explains the awakening dimension of Paul's religious experience. The religious experience that the mediated liberation model (m. 4) expresses is the awakening to the true Self/Christ as a religious experience. The center of this theology is the perichoresis between Christ and believers. The experience is the functional union within each other. While the mediated salvation model (m. 3) understands the event of the cross as the past event for the forgiveness of sin, the mediated liberation model (m. 4) brings up the present experience of the presence of Jesus Christ. He attempts to rediscover the awakening form in model 4 from the perspective of field theory theology.

In sum, regarding Yagi's structural study of the New Testament, there are two types of salvation stories depicted by personification language: the mediated salvation model (m. 3) and the mediated liberation model (m. 4). Both propose faith in Christ as Savior, but each of them points to a different way of the work of Christ: the past event of forgiveness of sin and the present reality of Christ joined with believers. Model 4 is compatible with the field theory language in that the faith form of Christ present should be actualized in one's own experience of awakening. Not until faith in Christ as liberator resonates can one enact one's own faith. Here, to understand this model, Yagi enlists a complementary language form. That is what Yagi learns from the Buddhist tradition: the language of field theory. This language makes it possible to approach the double experience of Jesus Christ in the New Testament. Revelation and awakening are not contradictory but complementary: Christ's revelation *to* us soku our awakening to Jesus Christ *in* us. Revelation and awakening are not identical, but they are not separable. They are not one but two. Therefore, they are one and two. This is the logic of soku.

Yagi finds in Paul's model 4 a clear compatibility between personification theology (model 4) and field theory theology. The tension that exists between them is the presence of Christ in Paul's existence. The life and death of believers are understood in the light of Jesus's life, death, and resurrection in model 4. It proclaims Christ's liberation from sin, death, law, and evil. Jesus Christ is revealed *to* Paul as the one who accomplishes liberation. However, the revelation becomes revelation to Paul with his awakening *in* Christ, the presence of Christ. Field theory theology takes it into account the lifting up of the simultaneous experience of faith in Christ soku awakening Christ in us. The simultaneous relationship between model 4 and field theory theology in Paul enables Yagi to clarify Paul's understanding of the law that is supported by the simultaneous dynamics of faith in Christ and awakening to Christ.

Law and Ethics

The main difference between the mediated salvation model (m. 3) and the mediated liberation model (m. 4) appears in terms of the treatment of the law in Paul. The mediated salvation model (m. 3) puts forward "disapproval for offense against law." In this context, Paul states, "There is no one who is righteous, not even one" (Rom 3:10), and "even Gentiles are not excluded" (Rom 2:13–15). Therefore, everyone needs to be forgiven only by the atoning death of Jesus Christ. The model presupposes obedience to law as good. The salvation that is grounded on this atonement can be expressed as an objective truth, whether one understands it or not. However, this theology about the cross raised the other arguments among the early Christians when it was said that those who had been forgiven by the atonement of Christ could stay in sin (Rom 6:1–15). Paul refutes this affirmation of the offense against law (Rom 6:2), but the mediated salvation model (m. 3) cannot persuade people of this argument. The biggest difficulty that the mediated salvation model (m. 3) brings about is the way of dealing with transgressions against the law after conversion.[15] This model deals with shortcomings of ethics in people.

Therefore, Paul needs something to persuade people about this issue. Yagi finds that Paul deals with the law not on basis of the mediated salvation model (m. 3) but the mediated liberation model (m. 4). Model 4 implies the absolute negation in terms of law; it disapproves of offense against and obedience to the law. What is at stake is the conversion of the subject, whether he or she obeys the law or not. Yagi summarizes what Paul represents in terms of law from the perspective of field theory theology:

> The position of the 'mere ego' must be replaced. This position, where the mere ego is willing to legitimize the ego alone, can be overcome by the replacement with the ultimate subject of Christ, that is, by the conversion that the whole person accepts the life of Christ. It is conversion of the subject from the mere ego to the ego awakened to the Self.[16]

---

15. This conflict appears between Aberald's moral theory and Anselm's satisfaction theory.

16. Ibid., 156.

The "disapproval of even obedience to law" has to be spoken from the awakening to the Self/Christ. Thinking of Paul's teaching about reconciliation, Yagi questions how Paul came to a new perspective of law and proclamation of the reconciliation between Jews and Gentiles. He assumes that Paul had a religious experience that is equal to the ego awakened to the self (*jikaku*). It appears in Paul's texts, among which "Christ in me" (Gal 2:19) is representative. In Galatians, Paul succinctly tells us that his apostolicity is granted only "through Jesus Christ and God the Father," neither by human commission nor human authority (Gal 1:1). It depends on the revelation, whose content is "the apocalypse of Jesus."[17]

According to Howard C. Kee, this saying of his fundamental conviction of the revelation of Jesus Christ from God belongs to "private revelations," not public and exterior reception of revelation like Acts expresses in chapters 9, 22, and 26. In other words, the revelation Paul received cannot be dissolved into any objective and external evidence. Rather, Paul returns his religious experience to his language of the letters: "Christ in me." Yagi finds the structure of faith in these passages in Paul's expression of the revelation. He argues that if readers do not consider that the language of revelation retains the structure of the religious experience of the ego awakened to the Self/Christ, they are dissolved into the conventional meaning of language: objectification of awakening without awakening. The language of Christ in me is not an objective or substantial language possible to prove but a representative language to be resonated. If the reader cannot resonate with the religious experience, the text cannot be decoded. It is similar to the way it is for those who do not understand music—to them, the piece of music is merely noise.

Yagi contends that Paul did not stand against the existence of the law but against the performance of the law. When the texts of the law fall apart from the event of revelation, they are performed as the conventional system of knowledge and language, such as juridical prescriptions or moral lists. This inclination toward performance created a wall between human beings and the divine intention of unity. Therefore, the very reason for the wall between us does not come from the difference of religion, whether Judaism, Christianity, or other; rather, it comes from the gap between the inherent nature that lives with a system of ideas and the depth of humanity, the world, and God. In other words, Yagi's theology asks, "On the basis of what and from what should the law be treated?"

---

17. Kee, "The Conversion of Paul," 48–61.

Paul's perspective of the law followed his experience of the revelation of Jesus Christ, which has not dissolved into our language system or identified with our semantic system of meaning. This religious experience pushed him to advocate for community for all. He identified the resurrected Lord with the crucified Jesus. The experience of this encounter functions to unite Paul with others. On the basis of the unity of Paul with Christ, he claims the unity between human beings. Because of this awakening, we can "live with holy Spirit" (Rom 8:4). On the basis of this conversion, Paul also speaks about the body as "God's temple" (1 Cor 2:16) or "a temple of the Holy Spirit" (1 Cor. 6:19), and he says that Christ lives in believers (Rom 8:9-10; Gal 2:20). Then he recognizes the church when he says, "You are the body of Christ and individually members of it" (1 Cor. 12: 27).

In these passages, the cross of Jesus Christ is not merely the atoning work but the event to show Christ's victory over the power of sin and death. It is understood as the "first fruits," which makes it possible for believers to anticipate Christ's victory in their lives. Believers accept model 4 by experiencing and participating in the story of the victory of Jesus Christ in their own lives. The model makes Paul confess that the subject of his mission is not him, but Christ: "I worked harder than any of them—though it was not I, but the grace of God" (1 Cor 15:10). Then, on the basis of this theology, he speaks about sanctification: "If anyone is in Christ, there is a new creation" (2 Cor 5:17; c.f. Gal 6:15). The language of field theory theology is spoken here by the language of personification theology. But Paul, by default, grasps the perichoretic relationship between the Father and the Son and between God and human beings in his personification language.

Here, Paul finds that the true subject is not Paul but Christ. This cannot be understood substantially. Otherwise, the personality of Paul is gone. Rather, while Paul remains Paul and he lives in his own ego, Paul is awakened to his true subject within him. It is Christ who lives and works within Paul. This is an event of the recovery of the authentic subject. This is what Yagi calls the ground experience of Christianity. Without this awakening to the primal fact, any model of the personification theology from model 1 to model 4 falls into superficial interpretation, or worse, it falls into Christian absolutism in the connection with objective truth. Field theory theology expresses this religious experience directly. I have already explored how the present reality of Christ works in a liberative perspective in chapter 1. Westhelle, like Yagi, particularly develops an incredible disposition of a theology of the cross in terms of the treatment of Jesus with "law that kills." The *epistemic key* depicts Jesus's subversive solidarity with those who suffer, by reason of which Jesus's ministry resonates with those who speak truth boldly in terms of *parrhesis*. In the case of Yagi, while concentrating on the same point of "law that kills," he moves forward to the inner liberative element of the Christ as liberator. That is the emancipation from within oneself.

LIBERATION AND CHRIST IN THE LIGHT OF THE SELF

According to Buddhism, suffering is a basic human condition and cannot be reduced to individual sin-guilt causality or to socio-political oppression. Life is full of suffering. That is the dimension of cosmic suffering. The deep root of human suffering comes from cosmic suffering. Viewed from the perspective of cosmic suffering, a human being is entangled with alienation from the whole universe. When Yagi reflects on Buddhist tradition, he finds the depth of human agony that pervades humanity. In a paper, he introduces two interpretations of the legend of the young Gautama, who went out of the four gates of his castle and saw the pain of life.[18] The one interpretation is well known. He left his status as a prince to search for freedom from pain. Another is that, when he saw the pain of life outside the gates, he also found "irrational self-assertion," which made silly men believe that they could be an exception and escape the suffering of life the others took on.

The problem in the first case is the painfulness of life itself. He thinks that people can find a solution through politico-economic revolution or by medical innovations. However, the second one is silly arrogance, by which they avoid compassion for the sufferer. The fundamental problem is to estrange the ego by substantializing the ego itself. Yagi finds the cause of this human problem in this absolutization. While learning the Buddhist philosophical understanding of suffering, he came to realize that the cause of suffering comes from his own ego in a Buddhist manner. However, the causality of the ego cannot be reduced to one's own individuality. Yagi is also aware that the human ego is a socio-cultural product nurtured by its system of language/knowledge when he thinks of law in the New Testament. Thus, liberation from the ego bound to the system

---

18. Yagi, "Christ and Buddha," 25–26.

of knowledge should be sought for the awakening to the true self, which is prevented by the ego. Considering the bondage between ego and social language/knowledge, Yagi sharpens the perspective of egoism.

Apart from the problem of egocentrism in general, he ponders the other problem of ego from the structural study of the New Testament. Generally, egocentrism is considered as an immoral attitude or behavior, parallel to transgressing the law. However, the egocentrism that Yagi clarifies from the study is defined as "that which recognizes only one's own ego as absolute."[19] The importance of this notion of egoism prompts concern about "moral and religious egocentrism." This type of egoism in connection with the law can be reinforced by accomplishing obedience to the law. It fills the moral requirement to serve others by following a moral code. The problem is that any activity ultimately results in establishing one's own ego, not religious truth. The deepest problem of egoism lies in the fact that it cannot take otherness into account. It is the central criticism of Jesus to Pharisaism in the New Testament.

As I explored the triple otherness that Yagi presents, this other is not only the otherness of God and neighbors but also the otherness of subject. The encounter with otherness within the subject paradoxically means the encounter with the true subject (Zen) or "Christ in me." The other aspect of the moral and religious egoism is to prevent us from meeting otherness and losing our real subject. For Yagi, the ego cannot take otherness as otherness; only the Self/Christ can do it. Regarding the subjectivity, the Self/Christ considers the subject to be the embodied self-constituent of spirit, soul, and body (*shintai-teki Jiko*):

> A human being is merely neither spirit nor reason, but *shintai* (the wholeness). *Shintai* means not "physical body." *Shintai* means the wholeness including heart, and the ego is originally just a part of the wholeness which functions consciously. . . . *Shintai* is a part of the world, a part of the sentient beings, and also personality which shares life with other personalities. Awakening means to awake to, to affirm and to wish this fact.[20]

For anyone to be emancipated from the cycle of this egoism, he or she should be awakened to the Self/Christ. This is the starting point for liberation from the dominant, conventional system of knowledge that Yagi proposes. The problem is not whether one should transgress the law

19. Yagi, *Structure of New Testament Thought*, 179.
20. Ibid., 11.

here. Rather, one is asked from which one direction one takes the law seriously, the ego or the self? Once one arrives at the limits of one's own knowledge, speculation, and performance of conventional knowledge, one comes to emptiness. The emptiness is not nothingness but the fullness of true self within the subject. The awakening to the self is equal to the awakening to true self in Zen Buddhism.

Yagi identifies the true self with what Christians call Christ. The connection between the awakening to the true self and faith in Christ is complementary in his own religious experience. He is convinced that the awakening to the true self can coexist with faith in Christ in Christianity. Regarding the triple encounter of the other, he argues that Christian faith brings about *I-Thou* encounter but also ego-self encounter in terms of "Christ in me." It is to replace the ego with the Self/Christ as the center of the subject. It is the conversion from the mere ego to the ego awakened to the self.

The Mere Ego and the Ego Awakened to the Self

Yagi calls the image of human beings who are awakened to the natural relationship between God, others, and the world "the ego awakened to the Self (*jikaku*)" on the basis of his field theory theology. This is a term contrasting with "the mere ego." The distinction between the Self and the ego derives from Japanese distinctions of human entity: self (*jiko*) and ego (*jiga*). According to Yagi, the mere ego is the "I" that we usually identify with who we are. The mere ego is not conscious of the Self within the subject. The ego is the ego based on human reason and the subject who thinks, perceives, and governs the subject's behavior.

However, Yagi argues that the true subject of a human being is not the mere ego. A human being is the whole person (body, mind, and soul or spirit). A human being cannot be reduced into spirit or reason. The ego is a part of the whole person, and it is not reversible. Yet, it is the case that human beings are willing to believe that the ego is the core of the subject who controls the other parts of the whole person. That is the inherent nature of the ego rooted in human reason. However, for Yagi, it is not about the ego but about the whole person, about which Paul teaches, "You are God's temple and that God's spirit dwells in you" (1 Cor 3:16). Accordingly, it is not the mere ego (human reason) but the whole person through which one comes to know God. The perception that the ego (human reason) becomes aware of God comes from the direct and unmediated human experience of God through the whole person. The relationship between subject and object cannot be divided completely here. Rather the relationship between the ego and the true Self (Christ) follows Takizawa's formulation of "inseparable, non-identical, and irreversible."

Yagi's idea about the ego awakened to the Self can be argued in connection with salvation. Yagi presents two types of salvation in the New Testament through his structural analysis of the New Testament. Just as I explored in previous sections, each representative form of the two salvation types is the "salvation through faith in the forgiveness of sin through the atoning work of Jesus Christ" and the "salvation through the awakening to 'Christ in me.'" Like Abe's distinction, Yagi calls the former the religion of *faith* and the latter the religion of *awakening*. The crucial difference between Abe and Yagi lies in the fact that while Abe distinguishes between faith and awakening from a Buddhist perspective against a Christian-Western perspective, Yagi proposes a religious type of *awakening* as one of the original religious experiences of Christianity. Yagi's main theological agenda is to recover the tradition of awakening in Christianity.

Taking the Pauline confession of "Christ in me," Yagi finds a double awakening. On the one hand, Paul's experience resonates with the *I* experience as the whole person in which the ego is awakened to something that cannot be recognized through the mere ego (human reason). On the other hand, the awakening to "Christ in me" is the perception that Christ is working within me, for Paul is perceived as a real subject. In this understanding, Christ is not the revelation at-one-moment in the life and death of Jesus, but the event happened in Paul's at-one-moment's life. If it is the case, and Christ is the subject of Paul, is Paul Christ? Yagi does not allow identifying Paul with Christ in a substantial manner. Otherwise, Paul would become Christ and Paul's existence would be gone. Rather, Yagi calls the unity between Christ and Paul the *functional union with Christ* (*sayou-itsu*). Paul is the field in which God (Christ in Paul) works, and also God (Christ in Paul) is the action that makes Paul a real subject. This is the point of contact between field theory theology and Zen Buddhism. Yagi introduces a story to explain the "whole secret of Zen."

One day, Ungan (a Chinese Zen master; 780?–841) made tea. His friend Dogo (769–835) came to him and asked:

- Dogo: For whom are you making tea?
- Ungan: There is the One who wants tea.
- Dogo: Why do you not let him make tea?
- Ungan: Fortunately, I am here.

Yagi heard this story from his interlocutor, the Zen master Akizuki Ryumin. According to Akizuki, this story derived from the conversation between young Ungan and his great Zen master Hyakujo (720–814). Hyakujo was well known by his saying: "If I do not work a day, I do not eat that day." This is the conversation between them:

- Ungan: For whom are you working every day so hard?
- Hyakujo: There is the One who needs that.
- Ungan: Why do you not let him work?
- Hyakujo: He cannot do daily work for himself.[21]

Yagi receives a great deal of insight from these stories, which help him to understand Paul's experience of Christ:

> It is interesting to see how Christ in Paul parallels "the One" in the Zen dialogue. Paul says, "For I will not venture to speak of anything except what Christ has wrought through me to win obedience from the Gentiles, by word and deed . . . (Rom. 15:18)." The mission of Paul is surely his own work. . . . If we had asked Paul, "Why do you preach the gospel?" Paul would answer, "Because Christ needs that." And if we had further asked him, "Why do you not let Christ himself preach the gospel?" He would say, just as Ungan and Hyakujo did, "Christ alone cannot preach the gospel and fortunately I am here" . . . . Christ, or "the One" works through the ego which has been awakened to it.[22]

Field theory theology makes it possible to talk about God relationally and functionally, not substantially. The relationship between Christ and Paul is not one, not two. Field theory theology avoids confusing Paul with Christ. Christ becomes immanent with us, but at the same time, beyond us. Christ represents our reality of trans-individuality (*cho-ko*): Christ in me soku I in Christ. Here Yagi challenges Christian absolutism, which is rooted in the identification between Jesus and Christ substan-

---

21. Yagi, "Christ and Buddha," 41–42.
22. Yagi, "What Can Claim Absoluteness?" 34.

tially. Jesus is the one who embodied this trans-individual reality. This notion comes to deal with revelation as religious experience. Because of this identification, Yagi scarcely mentions the term revelation. Revelation always happens within human perception. Yet, it does not mean that revelation is dependent on human ability or the human condition. It is possible to discuss divine existence or revelation apart from our human experience, but it is hardly meaningful to Yagi. There is no objective revelation. Everything in terms of revelation is interpreted as the expressive form of religious experience. Without an awakening, revelation does not make any sense and even joins hands with the exclusive-absolute claim of Christianity in relation to other religions.

The Interpretation of the Narrative from the Perspective of the Awakened Ego to the Self

First, Yagi argues, Jesus's disciples did not come to awakening to the life of Jesus until they confronted the death of Jesus. Their experience of the death and resurrection of Jesus within them is thoroughly the transformation of their epistemology for God, the world, and the self/others through the awakening to the Self/Christ. The resurrection of the crucified Jesus brought about something like Great Death and Great Life in terms of Zen Buddhism. Second, the awakening to the Self is understood to discover the true *I*, the true subject. But Yagi distinguishes between the Self/Christ and the true *I*. Just as Zen Buddhism claims, the Self is trans-individual reality (cho-ko in Japanese). The Self is the field where God's working pervades. Therefore, at the same time that one realizes the Self/Christ within oneself, one also realizes that the Self/Christ is beyond oneself, but at the same time, there is Self/Christ apart from individuals. Therefore, the awakening to the self is awakening to otherness within oneself. It makes us recognize our co-dependent reality to each other. This reality confronts the mere ego that thinks of itself as an independent entity, like *cogito ergo sum*.

The encounter of Christ retains its double structure. Christ is revealed *to* one, and simultaneously, Christ is awakened in the one. The former confronts the one, and the latter comes from within the one. The revealed Christ is also the Christ awakened as the Self by subject. While the salvation of the atoning work of Christ is understood diachronically, field theory theology understands salvation synchronically. Our ignorance is attributable to the unknown working of God within us.

Paradoxically, Yagi affirms that any human being has the potential to be awakened to the Self. Regarding Christology, Jesus is a historical human being. However, talking about Jesus as the one who was awakened to the working of God from within, Yagi can identify the religious life of Jesus with the religious experience of Paul. On this point of religious experience, Yagi does not qualitatively distinguish Jesus's religious experience from that of Paul and Gautama Buddha. All of them are those who lived with the true Self/Christ as their subjects. The Christ takes priority over any historical figure. The relationship between the subjects of Jesus, Paul, and Gautama and Christ/Self is irreversible.

CONCLUSION

Yagi's theological context is to be a Christian in a Buddhist context. He does not sell out his Christian identity or local identity. It is, rather, impressive that he seeks common ground between Christianity and Buddhism in academic dialogue. He puts himself in the "front structure between Christianity and Buddhism," in a place where each religion intersects the other. Because of his context, at an axis between both religions, his contextual theology cannot help but be intercontextual. I will attempt to review field theory theology in the encounter with the other contextual issues.

Contemplation or Action?

First of all, Yagi's contribution is to make sense of Christian faith in its Buddhist context from the perspective of the awakening. He realized, in dialogue with Zen Buddhism, that his intuitive encounter with the other is the realization of the other in a condition in which subject and object cannot be separated. The triple encounter with the other has no place other than subject. His *field theory* theology specifies what happens in the subject in the encounter with the other. The ego cannot assume the center of the subject because it is only reason's function to control information. Despite this fact, when the mere ego tries to enact itself as the center of subject, it causes relentless desiring and craving and results in the deepest dilemma. A human being is not merely ego but the whole person who carries embodiment. As the whole person, the subject is reborn when the subject is awakened to the action of God located in the center of the subject. The center is not the ego but the Self (the true self). The Self is the center of the subject and at the same time trans-individual. The subject is the field (or *Topos*) where God works, and at the same time, God is the ultimate subject of the whole person. Yagi attempts to clarify that this awakening to the Self is nothing other than Paul's experience of conversion: "Christ in me." It was a simultaneous event with faith in Christ as Savior. This field theory theology can respond to Knitter's question directed to Abe, in which he asks about the relationship between contemplation and action.

As I have already demonstrated, the dialogue between Abe and Knitter indicates the difference between *agapeic* Christianity and *gnostic* Buddhism. However, there is still room to transform each other through mutual interaction. Knitter infers his own hope behind the question of whether Buddhism and Christianity can cooperate to realize justice. When he asks about whether one should take contemplation or action, he considers that Christian contemplation tends to neglect action. He assumes that the same thing is said about Zen meditation. Yagi argues from field theory theology that Paul's awakening, which is compatible with model 4, presents a new understanding of the law: the double negation of transgression of the law and obedience to the law. What is at stake is the problem of the subject. What kind of subject addresses the treatment of law, the mere ego, or the ego awakened to the Self/Christ?

The problem of the subject cannot be simply reduced to an individual spiritual matter because it includes the social-political reaction of the subject. Everything hinges on the matter of the subject. The conversion from the mere ego to the ego awakened to the Self/Christ results in judging both contemplation and action. Yagi divides human subjects between the ego and the self. The Self is both individual and trans-individual. The subject, which awakens to the true subject, finds the action of God in its center, which integrates the whole person. Yagi understands Jesus's reign as God as the actualization that the Self actualizes individually and thus trans-individually.[23] God can be recognized as action within the subject. God is the ultimate subject, and at the same time, God is the action within us. The world is within the field of divine action. A human being is included in the field of action. Because of this "primordial fact," anyone can be awakened to the Self/Christ at any time and in any place. Thus, the ground of salvation lies in the cosmic awareness of the reign of God in field theory theology.

23. Yagi, "Buddha and Jesus."

This understanding is rephrased in Paul's passages like, "It is not I, but Christ who lives in me" (Gal 2:20). Because of this awakening, Yagi can accept the faith formula that the personification language puts forward. Neither contradicts the other. The personification language can express Paul's conversion in the form of *I-Thou* like this: Christ called him, sent him as an apostle, and committed his mission to him. Accordingly, the external calling from Christ to Paul in the personification theology and the internal calling from the Christ within the subject are faith experiences that happen simultaneously. In other words, God's calling in the I-thou relationship and the ego-self encounter with the other are simultaneous. From this awakening, Yagi argues that it is necessary not only to obey the law but also to transgress it. This notion responds to Knitter's question, contemplation, or action. If you contemplate or work for justice from the ego awakened to the Self/Christ, each of them is affirmed. If you do not, neither is acceptable.

Justification and Holy Spirit

Field theory theology challenges us to rethink our own tradition. As Yagi is aware, his claim of the simultaneous realization of faith and awakening is not to add something new to Christianity but to remind us of the depth of Christian tradition. One of them is his theological orientation regarding the Holy Spirit. Although the term "self" in self-awakening is misleading, Yagi thoroughly considers awakening as the work of the Holy Spirit. It is right that Drummond recognizes Yagi as "A God-focused believer."[24]

Interestingly, Daniel L. Migliore explores justification by faith in the section on the doctrine of the Holy Spirit.[25] He suggests the contemporary significance of justification by faith in the context of those who desperately crave the acceptance of self and absorb themselves in many kinds of addictions, such as drugs, money, work, leisure, and so on, in American society. There, people are driven by "the desire to 'make it,' to feel valued, accepted, and loved."[26] He is convinced that justification provides them with the acceptance of self on the ground of God's affirmation. He summarizes God's justification (acceptance) of those into the Trinitarian form of justification:

24. Drummond, "A Giant in Biblical Studies from the Far East."
25. Migliore, *Faith Seeking Understanding*, 235–9.
26. Ibid., 238.

> We are "somebodies" because God our creator and our redeemer says so. It is because we are creatures made in the divine image, because we are children of God, persons for whom Jesus Christ suffered, died, and was raised again, persons in whom the Spirit of God is at work—because of all this, we are somebodies. That is the basis of our dignity, our worth, our human rights, and our human responsibilities.[27]

Yagi's distinction between two types of theology/language illumines the typical personification language of this passage. Migliore speaks of the justification by faith in the I-thou relationship. God comes to those who fail to be justified as "external" Other through the Holy Spirit. From the perspective of field theory theology, I can say that the justification by faith, which is expressed by the personification language (God justifies them), is based on self-understanding or self-awakening. Migliore speaks these words from the conviction of those who experience God's justification within their subject. The seriousness of the addictions lies in the fact that the subject cannot recognize that he or she cannot take what he or she seeks from these objects of addiction. But how can he or she distinguish being justified by faith or by addictions? For those who do not resonate with justification by faith, it is not enough to say, "You are accepted by a power that is greater than you," because the place of the problem in this case lies not only in the agency of acceptance, but in the subject itself. Because the personification language takes the division between subject and others for granted from the beginning, it is difficult to question the division between the ego and the self in subject. Field theory theology examines the problem of the subject who desires, craves, and seeks justification or acceptance. It may be ambiguous to think about this issue in the case of addiction because anyone can understand that the objects of addiction have negative value. It is helpful to remind ourselves of Yagi's "moral and religious egoism."

This egoism can enslave the subject in the self-centered ego even through obeying law, and by the same token, even through serving God and neighbors. As long as the subject who desires acceptance remains the mere ego, he or she cannot distinguish whether the "acceptance" that he or she receives comes from God or from the many kinds of addiction. Field theory language can even say the "law addiction," "love addiction," "piety addiction," "justice addiction," and so on. The real distinction

---

27. Ibid., 239.

should be sought not outside the subject but inside. Unless the subject encounters the otherness within the subject, which makes the subject real, even justification by faith is in danger of falling into the prescriptive recommendation of belief: first human action, second divine action.

For Yagi, the realization of the awakening to the Self/Christ means the perfect realization of humanity and divinity within the subject. Humanization means the awakening to the fact that the center of subject is not the ego but the Self/Christ. Divinization means that the awakening is dependent on the work of Holy Spirit, which actualizes our true subjectivity. It should not be understood ontologically because it is realized by the functional union of God/Christ with the subject. Field theory theology claims the simultaneous occurrence of the encounter with the external other and the inner other. This theology thoroughly points out the confusion between the human work of "faith" and the divine work of "faith" without awakening to the Self/Christ. Because of the distinction of subject between the mere ego and the ego awakened to the Self/Christ, field theology is good at speaking about the facet of God who works internally within the subject: the Holy Spirit.

Despite this contribution, field theory theology brings another issue: Yagi does not mention faith as divine agency. While he argues that the Holy Spirit enables us to awake to Christ in ourselves, the combination of faith with the cross is understood in the combination of human belief with the atonement theory about the cross. The "faith" that he criticizes is synonymous with human belief or trust. From the identification of faith with belief, he understands that faith cannot be alone without awakening. However, a theology of the cross primarily understands faith as divine work within the subject. It is God's own work as a gift. Westhelle speaks of "faith desiring" from the cross, and Yagi speaks about the work of the Holy Spirit in the awakening ego. In both cases, God is the one taking action. Can we say that the faith of a theology of the cross is synonymous with Yagi's "justification by the awakening by the power of the Spirit"? How can I distinguish between faith and the Holy Spirit? Do I need it? The answer depends on the treatment of the cross.

Faith, Discipleship, and the Cross

While Fritsch-Oppermann appreciates Yagi's theology as the "interreligious hermeneutics of the Other," she also points out the absence of a theology of the cross in Yagi:

What many Western theologians see as a convergence with the theology of the cross is more of a structural convergence of the doctrine of *shunyata* with the doctrine of the cross. Yagi, at least, cannot maintain this convergence down to the deepest level in his theology.[28]

What Fritsch-Oppermann tries to sustain is the confession tradition that Jesus Christ is the resurrection of the crucified, which is rooted in the historical event. The theology of the cross is more than atonement theories and more than a sign. It is rooted in the cross event, that divine affirmation that pervades even in the depth of the cross and was revealed by the resurrection of the crucified Jesus. Luz also supports her idea by pointing to the simple fact that "in Christianity, the founder himself suffered," unlike gnostic religions, which teach that all suffering belongs to the world but you do not belong there.[29] Although it is too great an oversimplification, it is still helpful to sketch that Buddhism directly teaches liberation from the cross (suffering) and a theology of the cross starts with revelation from the cross. The cross that is nothing other than human cruelty and violence is revelation as the sign of divine commitment only in the sense of paradox. It is crucial to recognize this point in taking the line with the North American theologians of the cross in chapter 1. A theology of the cross sustains the memory embodied in the people who witnessed to the cross.

The cross they mentioned is the paradoxical revelation on the cross. For them, the cross is also a place where we cannot recognize any divine or graceful thing by our own ability. It is the end of human belief, which is the "faith" that Yagi criticizes. Here there is no room for human belief or human awakening. It is the moment of absence of human activity. Therefore, a theology of the cross is a kind of oxymoron, because they in the Bible, and we in particular, lose the knowledge of God at the place of the cross. The reason they lost their activity, whether *poiesis* or *praxis*, is not necessarily reduced to their problem of egoism. The narrative of the cross narrates the cosmic dimension of suffering that overwhelms individual spirituality, egoism, sinfulness, whatever. They, including Jesus, were overwhelmed by the darkness of sin, evil, and death. God can be spoken of only in a paradoxical way. I think the significance of Luther's hiddenness of God appears only in this context. This hiddenness is dif-

---

28. Fritsch-Oppermann, "Christian Existence in a Buddhist Context," 230.
29. Luz and Michaels, *Encountering Jesus & Buddha*, 102.

ferent from Abe's emptying God in terms of absolute Nothingness. The hidden God in the cross is the God who was incarnated in the suffering beyond our cognition. If we can say anything about faith in the place of faith, it is nothing other than something transcendent (divine).

These elements of a theology of the cross are outside Yagi's reflection, because they are historical and contingent. Therefore, Jesus's life, death, and ministry are transferred into the content of his religious thought. The cross is not necessary for awakening, and the resurrection is cut off from the event of the cross. Therefore, Fritsch-Oppermann disagrees with Yagi in this point: "For Christians, to perceive the truth of God means to perceive the truth of the cross, having both the courage to accept temporary truth and the humility to handle the doxology (of the cross) and assertion which is expressible in language."[30] Yagi's absence of a theology of the cross results from the fact that everything hinges on awakening to "Christ in me." In this regard, although he insists on faith soku awakening, I am suspicious of whether he accepts the divine agency of faith as well as the divine agency of awakening.

A theology of the cross sustains the historicity of any religious experience, whether awakening or faith. It is helpful to remember Westhelle's eloquent reconstruction of human activity in the Judeo-Christian tradition. He reconsiders the Aristoterian division of human art, *theoria*, *poiesis*, and *praxis*, in light of a theology of the cross. His purpose is to distinguish Judeo-Christian human arts in which divine art splits from Aristotelian confidential human art. Unlike Aristotelian theoria, the biblical theoria is intervened in by divine poiesis. The creation story in the Old Testament and resurrection in the New Testament together witness to divine poiesis, in which human arts halt and just witness to divine poiesis with feelings of awe and fascination.[31] That is the moment of theoria. Unlike the first divine poiesis in the creation story, the second poiesis in the resurrection story makes human beings feel *awe (tremendum)*. That is the second creation of Christ.

This is the reason why Fritsch-Oppermann and Luz hesitate to do theology without the cross. The "second story of poiesis (resurrection)" brings not only fascination but also a sense of awe. A theology of the cross starts with the second poiesis of the resurrection of the crucified. Faith brings the historical-eschatological perspective from this starting

30. Fritsch-Oppermann, "Christian Existence in a Buddhist Context," 234–5.
31. Westhelle, *The Scandalous God*, 132–6.

point. The claim on the historical cross is not aimed at the dogmatic or exclusive claim of Christian absolutism. Rather, "The goal of confessing faith is discipleship,"[32] which leads to orthopraxis:

> The relative manifestation of the absolute within the relative, the incarnation of the divine mystery, we can perhaps say, leads us unavoidably into practice. Practice means that we proclaim the truth with eschatological reservation.[33]

The absence of reflection on the cross raises a different issue. It is the same as what John Cobb, Moltmann, and Keller ask Abe. How does field theory theology take historicity and ethics into consideration in the sense of responsibility for historical event? Asserting the work of the Holy Spirit, not the work of faith, the ground of salvation is identified with the cosmic awareness of the absolute identification between the self and other. However, there still remains Christian uniqueness, the historical memory of Jesus's life, ministry, and the cross, even if dogmatism and absolutism are excluded. There is no kenosis of Christ without the embodiment of the cross. From here, Westhelle considers the function of theology as keeping an "empathetic memory" in the sense of Benjamin. It also opens the possibility to link Jesus's naming ministry with others beyond religions who engage in the mission of *"parrhesia."* Solberg challenges a dominant epistemology and suggests "strategic objectivity" and grounds the activity of knowing in everyday life. Thomsen relates "divine metacosmic love" with the embodiment of Jesus's spirituality in his ministry.

Luther's theology of the cross is foundational for these constructive theologies. The revelation is nothing out of our embodiment in history and time. It is also the work of God that can be sensed only through one's own life and death. The work of God is a "becoming process" rather than "primodinal fact" from the beginning. Luther is aware of the sheer temporality of our knowledge of God. He does not regard theology as a study of principles, but as a "study of history and experience."[34] I do not think that this idea from the cross excludes the contingency of the cross, because of which Yagi is indifferent to the cross in his reflection.

---

32. Fritsch-Oppermann, "Christian Existence in a Buddhist Context," 233.
33. Ibid.
34. Bayer, *Theology the Lutheran Way*, 29.

Rather, because of this contingency, because of the at-one-moment, anyone who lives in this contingent world can receive divine affirmation, justification, and acceptance in spite of our at-one-moments. One difficulty of field theory theology is that many of us do not live in the awakening de facto. According to Westhelle, a theology of the cross is a theology for those who are in the moment of absence—the moment of absence soku the moment of faith desiring.[35] While Yagi takes the reality of egoism seriously, the liberative perspective is willing to relate with the cosmic suffering going beyond the socio-political dimension of suffering, which cannot be reduced to either individual agony or the socio-political dimension of suffering. Abe and Yagi converge in their existential solution despite their recognition that Buddhism sheds light on the cosmic dimension of suffering. A theology of the cross can go further to touch on Paul's awareness that suffering pervades the cosmic dimension in Romans 8. The paradoxical reality of God between the moment of absence and the moment of faith takes the perspective of cosmic suffering.

In other words, in the moment of the absence of our awakening and faith, faith desiring works through us. Model 4 in Paul does not necessarily enact the dimension of faith without awakening if one understands faith as a gift from God. Can we say that "Christ in me" is actualized even before we are awakened to this? This is also the other side of what Knitter, a liberation theologian, asks Abe. This acceptance is the acceptance of the theology of the cross that makes us understand Jesus's cry on the cross, "My God, my God, why have you forsaken me?" (Mark 14:34). Even if we encounter the moment of the absence of God, we are convinced that we are in divine mercy and solidarity because of the cross of Jesus Christ. The cross is not merely a symbol but the embodiment of the crucified. The world, cross, and subject are not merely the place of the work of God; rather, it is a becoming process heading toward an eschatological consummation. In the encounter with the cosmic *dukkha*, a theology of the cross opens to the cosmic Christology. This is the topic of the next chapter.

---

35. The meaning of *soku*.

5

A Theology of the Cross in Encounter with Cosmic *Dukkha*

INTRODUCTION: MINJUNG CONTEXT

IN THIS BOOK, I have set up three interactive perspectives to advance my argument: Luther's theology of the cross, contextual theology, and intercontextual theology. Contextual theology makes it possible to do theology in a particular location. In the light of contextual theology, Luther's theology of the cross serves to suspend the context of Christian tradition and the context of contemporary theologians. Finally, contextual theology also implies the necessary consequence to open itself to other contextual theologies. A theology of the cross accelerates the compatibility of contextual theology with intercontextual dialogue. I will illuminate next how Paul Chung's theology of the cross exemplifies the dynamic waving process of these methodological features in an Asian context of the cross. I will also show that this enables him to propose a comprehensive theology of the cross, as his thesis states, "Asian theology of the cross pursues divine suffering in personal, social, political, cosmological realms and also in other religious dimensions."[1]

Minjung Theology from the Context of Asian Liberation Theology

Minjung theology is a "contextual theology in solidarity with the social biography of the suffering people in Korea."[2] Chung is in line with this minjung theology. His teacher, Ahn Byung-Mu, was one of the initiators of minjung theology during the military dictatorship in Korea during

---

1. Chung, *Martin Luther and Buddhism*, 188.
2. Chung, "Relevance of Martin Luther," 40.

the 1970s and 1980s. Although I have already shown how Thomsen transforms the framework of a theology of the cross from the individual-spiritual dimension to a more corrective dimension of suffering, Ahn Byung-Mu is also critical of a kind of a theology of the cross that focuses on individual salvation. He pursues a theology of the cross in a way that makes a complementary synchronization between the embodied suffering of the cross and the massive suffering of *minjung* (people). He identifies minjung (people-mass suffering) with *ocholos* in the Markan usage, which indicates Jesus's followers, rather than *laos* in the Lukan usage.[3] Jesus is not merely the Messiah for them, but in them: "Jesus is not an individual hero for the minjung but one of them in sharing the same fate and destiny with them which is the true meaning of Christ's kenosis and suffering."[4] Like liberation theology, in the situation of the social-political situation, they came to find a solidarity Christology with the poor/oppressed.

When Chung reviews minjung theology in the broader Asian context, he agrees with Aloysius Pieris's view that Asian theology has two perspectives: "Asian massive poverty and Asian richness of religiosity."[5] It is important to pay attention to the point of contact between Korean minjung theology and Pieris's Asian liberation theology. First, the Asian religions have much "in common concerning spiritual, personal, moral, and social life in a humanitarian-cosmological view."[6] Second, regarding the direction of liberation, Asian culture has a long history in terms of Buddhism liberation. In this tradition, "To overcome *dukkha* is not restricted to the historical domain, but is connected to self-emptying transcendence."[7] Suffering and poverty in context are not merely issues that can be overcome through the class struggle for liberation; rather, theology should approach "other spiritual dimensions of detachment and a religious spirituality of kenosis in destroying and transcending craving paradoxically so as to become the poor."[8] Thus, while Chung sustains the theological perspective of minjung theology, he still seeks a theology of religions that makes it possible to work with liberation theology comple-

---

3. Ahn, "Jesus and *Ochlos*," 33–50.
4. Chung, *Luther and Buddhism*, 171.
5. Pieris, "The Buddha and the Christ."
6. Chung, *Luther and Buddhism*, 3.
7. Ibid., 189.
8. Ibid., 189.

A Theology of the Cross in Encounter with Cosmic Dukkha   117

mentarily. Because minjung theology starts its theological reflection with the massive suffering of people facing socio-political oppression, this theology initially touches on their own religiosity, which forms their way of life in the context of political oppression. Kim Kyung-Jae, another teacher of Chung, advanced the other side of minjung theology. Kim claims that as long as minjung theology is faithful to its own context, it brings itself to a point of fusion with diverse Asian religious traditions.

Minjung Liberation and Asian Spirituality

Doing contextual theology in East Asia requires paying attention to peculiar conditions. Just as Paul Chung always insists, Asian theological practice is in the contexts of immense poverty and immense religiosity. Although Korean minjung theology develops liberation theology in an Asian context, it also develops its own theological perspective in an inter-religious context because minjung cannot be classified by established concepts like Christianity or Buddhism. Reflecting on these contexts, Kim Kyoung-Jae develops a hermeneutics of mission theology in an East Asian context.

    Kim is aware of a paradigm shift from the traditional Western theology of mission toward a local context. The locality in East Asia is represented as a "more hermeneutical and experiential theology of mission in respect to our global context."[9] He does not advance a theological program with either/or choices. Rather, he seeks a creative encounter between Korean, East Asian culture and Christian tradition.[10] We find a common tendency in Asian religion and culture, in spite of great diversity, which Ariarajah observes, that culture and religion cannot be isolated and even religions are inextricably entangled with each other in the long history of Asia. When he recognizes the interconnections of cultures and religions, he says that culture is "like the flesh, blood and soul of the shaping of the community."[11] I recognize that the intercontextual necessity of contextual theology cannot qualify as an interlocutor

---

    9. Kim, "Christianity and Culture," 147.

    10. Ibid., 147. Kim defines East Asian in his theological work: "Geographically to Chinese speaking countries, specifically countries, such as China, South-Korea, Japan and Vietnam. These are cultural communities which are composed of multi-religious societies and have shared the great religious cultural legacies of Buddhism, Confucianism, Taoism and indigenous religions for over 2000 years."

    11. Ibid., 149.

within the Christian domain. He believes culture cannot be separated from religion. When a religion is mentioned, it forms the wholeness including diverse religions, like Buddhism, Confucianism, Taoism, and other indigenous religions. They cannot be easily isolated from each other. This is the complexity of Asian religiosity. Kim Kyung-Jae makes each of them encounter the Christian faith tradition creatively. In this regard, he is critical of the conventional missionary work in East Asia because many missionaries are afraid of syncretism and cut the wholeness of culture and religiosity into pieces and input Christianity as a supreme religion into the wholeness. As a consequence, Christianity loses the point at which it could otherwise meet and engage others, because:

> Western missionaries were not able to distinguish from the gospel a historical form of Christendom . . . they absolutized their conception of Christianity forming its specific historical form.[12]

To replace syncretism, he introduces the "hermeneutical fusion of horizon" into Asian missiology. That is not just the "fusion of horizons" in the sense of the interpretation of the texts (Hans-Georg Gadamer) but of "the life experience" of people who live in East Asia:

> East Asian culture can be understood as the history of an on-going process in which a 'complementary weaving process' of truth experience has occurred. . . . East Asian history of culture must be understood as an integrating of the world's religions, such as Confucianism, Buddhism, Taoism, Islam, and Christianity.[13]

When doing theology in this diversity, one constructs one's own contextual theology, but at the same time, the contextual theology necessarily includes the other contextual theologies in the complex Asian tradition. Chung also seeks a "hermeneutical fusion of horizon" between Luther and Buddhism. In doing so, he addresses the Asian double theological issue: religiosity and poverty. His hermeneutical key is Luther's theology of the cross.

---

12. Ibid., 151. See also Schreiter, *New Catholicity*, 62–83; 84–97. Schreiter presents a different picture of the "Western" missiology about syncretism in reflection with current contextual theology.

13. Ibid., 154.

THE ASIAN PERSPECTIVE OF SUFFERING: COSMIC DUKKHA.

Luther's theology of the cross in the light of orthopraxis shows the challenge of suffering when it bears a liberative perspective. The theology of the cross goes beyond soteriology and presents the theology of struggle. The struggle is aimed to overcome its own individual and spiritual salvation and to challenge the social-structural evil and socio-political oppression. The cross is not merely a spiritual symbol of salvation but a "scandal" and a "stumbling block." For theologians of the cross, it is more crucial that the cross is the event in which God was incarnated in a particular time and space: Jesus of Nazareth. The liberative perspective of the cross explores the historical Jesus from his life to the cross in light of the resurrection of the crucified. That is, theology takes historicity and ethics into its perspective. In light of this liberative perspective, Luther's theology of the cross is an object to be criticized but also an object to be rediscovered. For the three North American theologians of the cross of chapter 1, what is at stake is to rediscover the depth of Christian tradition from the orthopraxis. As they show the presence of Christ as the power of liberation, minjung theology primarily views Jesus from the present reality of minjung (*ochlos* or suffering people): "the Jesus event is articulated with emphasis on its on-going occurrence in our daily lives."[14]

Chung opens a way for Asian people, who live in the double context of "poverty and religiosity," to find their own orthopraxis in "solidarity Christology" through his own background of minjung theology. This is a cosmic Christology in the encounter of cosmic dukkha in a Buddhist context. Here, a theology of the cross expands its own perspective into the Asian Buddhist perception of suffering, cosmic dukkha, through the Christ as liberator.

Buddhism is a practical religion that aims to liberate from suffering. It puts Buddha's Four Noble Truths into the central teaching. As Abe shows, the root of suffering lies in the impermanency of all sentient beings in the world (*samsara* world). According to the Four Noble Truths, first of all, we have to recognize that life is full of suffering (dukkha). Life is full of eight kinds of suffering in its cosmic view: birth, old, age, sickness, separation from one's beloved, being in the presence of those

---

14. Chung, *Luther and Buddhism*, 172. The quotation is related to a "pneumatological-synchronic interpretation" by Su Nam-Dong (1918–1984), one of the founding fathers of minjung theology.

you dislike, not getting what you desire, and the imbalance of the five aggregates. This is the reality of human beings who live in the samsara. Second, suffering is caused by craving or the thirst for sensory desires. Then, we are led to a recognition of liberation from suffering. Suffering can be stopped by the cessation of this craving (to nirvana). Finally, the way of liberation becomes clear, a nirvanic liberation through the practice of the Eightfold Path. The Eightfold Path includes right view, right thought, right speech, right action, right livelihood, right effort, right mindfulness, and right meditation. In comparison with the Western theological tradition in which suffering has been discussed in connection with sin against God, Buddhist suffering is inherently immanent and thus cosmic. The more we try to escape the dukkha, the more we are entangled with dukkha because the craving itself is the cause of suffering. The liberation from the suffering of dukkha is dependent on the practice of the Eightfold Path. But this is not a simple practice, because its purpose is to liberate ourselves from ourselves in the first place. It is enlightenment or awakening to *Sunyata* (emptiness or emptying).[15]

Fundamentally, Buddhism is a practical religion for liberation from suffering rooted in the human suffering reality. Unlike Abe's deconstructive approach that I explored in chapter 3, Chung seeks a constructive way in the encounter with Buddhism. Cosmic dukkha, which Chung uses, symbolically represents the understanding of the cosmic dimension of suffering. Here, the theology of the cross, in which Jesus is the one of self-emptying, encounters Asian-Buddhist enlightenment to absolute Nothingness.

CHRIST LIBERATOR SOKU COSMIC CHRIST

Luther in Asia

Paul Rajashekar has already set the current orientation of Lutheran theology in Asia in intercontextual dialogue.[16] He reflects on the past contour of Lutheran theological development and questions "Luther study" in Asia. They remain ambiguous, because, he thinks, these studies are

---

15. Ibid., 17. Chung summarizes *Sunyata* as, "To get out of this suffering it is decisive to attain complete emptiness, nirvana. . . . If originally everything is fundamentally empty, everything in the whole universe is the same substance, because the substance is empty. . . . The experience of the emptiness reveals the ultimate truth of the world."

16. Rajashekar, *Theology in Dialogue*, 1.

dependent on deductive methods, "translation," or a "restatement" of the past theological issues. Consequently, they inadequately reflect the current context of Asian theology. In order to break through this situation, he calls for a creative dialogue between Christian identity and Christian relevancy in Asia. Thus, dialogue is "not merely a method of discussion," but a "commitment to do theology in an inclusive way."[17] He shares a similar hope that Kim Kyoung-Jae presents through the "hermeneutical fusion of horizon." However, it is not easy to find a creative dialogue between sixteenth-century Wittenberg and the current Asian diversity of religious traditions, as it clearly was to find such diverse topics as Rajashekar proposes in a symposium.[18]

Kitamori works in this context of "God and gods in dialogue," in which the substantial transcendental, and personal God is not ultimate. Yagi opens a way to recognize the Ultimate that makes it possible for Christians and Buddhists to agree at the level of religious experience. However, neither is adequate to lift up the embodiment of suffering with revelation in the cross. Chung focuses on the connection between revelation and the embodiment of the cross in Luther's theology of the cross and moves forward toward the encounter with Buddhist cosmic dukkha.

Chung's understanding of Luther's theology of the cross follows the position that Luther's theology of the cross is a principle for constructing his entire theology since Loewenich presented his thesis at the beginning of the twentieth century. Justification comes through the cross event. God is hidden in the cross and meets sinners through the cross and justifies them. Just as Solberg clarifies, the epistemology of the cross brings about an "epistemological break" in the midst of life. The embodiment of the cross of Jesus is not separable from the embodiment of people's suffering. The theology of the cross is a kind of new epistemology that does not rely on an "objective" epistemology.

According to Chung, the most precious thing that the theology of the cross receives about the knowledge of God is the communication of attributes in Luther's Christology. Luther's communication of attributes provides theological ground for the "historical approach to God's suffering."[19] It is aimed at keeping the humanity of Christ connected to

17. Ibid., 8.
18. The subthemes that he proposes are: "God and gods in dialogue," "Scripture and scriptures in dialogue," "witnessing in dialogue," "dialogue in community," "ministry and theological education in dialogue," and "tradition in dialogue."
19. Chung, *Luther and Buddhism*, 134.

the incarnation of the Son of God. Chung calls this Christology "from below." The doctrine of the communication of attributes was not a new one in Luther's age. Luther's newness lies in his intention to use this doctrine. This doctrine has played an important role to explain that Christ is truly human and truly divine. While the Antiochene School emphasized the distinction between divinity and humanity, the Alexandrian School sought the integrity between those attributes in Christ. Chung argues that Luther develops a dynamic communication from divinity to humanity in following the footsteps of the Alexandrian tradition, as represented by these words:

> It is correct to say that the Son of God was crucified and died for us. But if someone objects that the deity cannot suffer and die, we reply that this is true, but yet because the deity and the humanity in Christ are one person, therefore, on account of such personal union the scripture attributes to the deity whatever belongs to the humanity and vice versa.[20]

Unlike the church fathers, Luther's communication of attributes is intended to talk about God, who is willing to communicate about himself with the suffering of humanity through the second person of the truly human and the truly divine. When this communication of attributes meets the Asian cosmic dukkha, the nature of the Christological question changes from Hellenistic, whether God can suffer, to Asian, how God embraces cosmic dukkha, and thus, people's life in cosmic dukkha.

From the Communication of Attributes through the Ubiquity of Christ into Cosmic Christ

Chung grasps Luther's theological development from the communication of attributes into the real presence of Christ and the ubiquity of Christ in light of his theology of the cross. He argues that Luther's theology of the cross pervades his later development, especially in the controversy about the Eucharist.[21] When one discusses Luther's theology of the cross in the framework of atonement theory, one can discern that Luther's theological discourse is influenced by Anselm's atonement theory. On the other hand, it has become clear that Luther's atonement

---

20. Ibid., 140. The original source of this quotation is: Luther, "Confession Concerning Christ's Supper," 210–1.

21. Chung, *Luther and Buddhism*, 179–80.

A Theology of the Cross in Encounter with Cosmic Dukkha

theory was inherited from the "classical type" that can be traced back to Irenaeus. Although we cannot say that Luther's theology of the cross is simply grounded in the classical model (Christ as the Victor), it is worth remembering his own context of the battle against scholasticism, which took the satisfaction theory of Anselm as its own system.[22]

What is at stake in Luther's battle against scholasticism is to recover the liberative and cosmic Christology. The Christology helps Luther emphasize the real presence of Christ and the ubiquity of Christ. Christ is seen through the cosmic frame from incarnation through resurrection into eschatological consummation in the doctrine of recapitulation.[23] In the controversy with Zwingli about the Eucharist, Luther rejected the right hand of God as a particular place and rather insisted on the ubiquitous presence of Christ. Arguing so, Luther claims this ubiquity is based on Christ as the Victor who participated in the human predicament and at the same time, allowed human beings to participate in his death and life. Suffering cannot do anything to block the presence of Christ. Through Christ, who was incarnated, died on the cross, descended into hell, was raised, and will come again as the eschatological Lord for all, those who live in cosmic dukkha encounter God through the ubiquitous Christ everywhere. Chung quotes Luther's own well-expressed words about the cosmic Christ:

> We believe that Christ, according to his human nature, is put over all creatures (Eph. 1:22) and fills all things . . . Not only according to his divine nature, but also according to his human nature, he is a lord of all things, has all things in his hand, and is present everywhere.[24]

In this cosmic Christology, the cross points to the fact that God affirms the suffering nature of this world, including humanity. The affirmation of the humanity of Christ, which coexists in the divinity, is the affirmation of creatures. This affirmation does not exclude death and

---

22. Pelikan, *Christian Tradition*, vol. 4, 162–3.

23. Pelikan considers Irenaeus's doctrine of recapitulation as the "most profound theological vindication in the second and third centuries of the universal Christian ideal of the imitation of Christ," and continues to summarize this doctrine: "the imitation of Christ by the Christian was part of God's cosmic plan of salvation which began with Christ's imitation of the Christian or, more precisely, with Christ's imitation of Adam." In Pelikan, *Christian Tradition*, vol. 1, 144.

24. Chung, *Luther and Buddhism*, 184, quoting from Luther, *Luther's Works*, 342.

suffering. Jesus's commissioning words, "I am with you always, to the end of the age" (Matt 28:20) can be heard as the present reality of the cosmic Christ in this context because the ubiquity of Christ pervades not only history but also the bottom of hell. Developing the cosmic Christology grounded on the theology of the cross, Chung contextualizes Moltmann's thesis of a theology of the cross into an Asian cosmic dukkha: "There is no suffering within this history of God which is not God's suffering; no death which has not been God's death in the history on Golgotha."[25] All can be known to us through the cross. The theology of the cross is foundational for Christology, the doctrine of God, and the doctrine of the Trinity. Reflecting on Luther's theological development through a theology of the cross, Chung arrives at the divine possibility with suffering people. The encounter of Luther's Christology based on the theology of the cross with cosmic dukkha enters a deeper dialogue with Buddhist Christology.

The Concrete Human Jesus and the Humanity of Christ

The Chalcedonian formula to clarify the relationship between the humanity and divinity of Christ is developed into the distinction and union between the humanity of Jesus and the humanity of Christ in the combinations of the doctrines of the enhypostasis and the anhypostasis. On the one hand, the enhypostasis designates Jesus as a human individual only in his unification with the Logos. The "individual concreteness in Jesus's human nature" seems to be lost in the doctrine, as the Antiochene School argued.[26] On this point, Buddhist Christology criticizes traditional Christology because it "has blocked to the possibility of independence of the human Jesus apart from the unity with the eternal logos of God."[27] While Chung shows sympathy for this criticism, he also shows the depth of Christian tradition by showing the combination of enhypostasis and anhypostasis.

> Leontius was able to hold that the humanity of Christ always exists in unity with his divinity, that is, in the eternal Logos. . . . the positive side of this teaching is called enhypostasis (existence

---

25. Moltmann, *The Crucified God*, 246.
26. Pannenberg, *Jesus—God and Man*, 340.
27. Chung, *Luther and Buddhism*, 318. He introduces this as a criticism from Takizawa Katsumi. Yagi agrees with Takizawa in this remark. See also Yagi, "What Can Claim Absoluteness?" 27–41.

in the Logos) in which Docetism is ruled out. The negative side is called anhypostasis (no other independent mode of existence apart from the eternal Logos) in which ebionitism is ruled out. The incarnated word is always the preexistent eternal Word, Son of God who became man (enhypostasis). Jesus the Man is always no other than the eternal Son of God (anhypostasis).[28]

Connecting enhypostasis with anhypostasis, Chung thinks that the incarnation in the man Jesus does not mean the abolishment of his humanity but the fulfillment in "union with the person, the hypostasis, of the Word of God."[29] Developing Barth's use of the combination, Chung further argues for the unification of the concrete human Jesus with the humanity of Christ. It is important to attend to the fact that Buddhist Christology insists that there is no qualitative differentiation between the concrete humanity of Jesus and that of all human beings. Chung thinks that Barth in his later thought brings a solution when he says, "In Jesus Christ it is not merely one human, but the *humanum* of all humans, which is posited and exalted as such to unity with God."[30] The humanity of Jesus is "inseparable" from, but "nonidentical" with and "irreversible" of, the humanity of Christ in union with the divinity of Christ. For him, the ubiquity of Christ should be thought of in the light of the Trinity and vice versa. Then, he can talk about the divine affirmation of all sentient beings in cosmic dukkha. It is the Christocentric affirmation of creatures in the light of Trinity. This moment of the all-embracing God of all sentient beings through the cosmic Christ is called the "motherly pain of God in begetting the Son in the Spirit." Through the affirmation of the humanity of Christ in the immanent Trinity from eternity, we can talk about the encounter of the suffering of God with cosmic dukkha.

This Christocentric way of affirming the cosmic dukkha cannot be separated from Luther's theology of *Anfechtung*. His knowledge of God, in terms of justification by faith, is an embodied knowledge in his life. When he speaks about the suffering of God in Christ based on the communication of attributes, his theology reaches a radical notion about God. When speaking about systematic theology, we have to deal with them separately, such as Christology, soteriology, the doctrine of God, the doctrine of Trinity, the doctrine of sacrament, and so on. However,

---

28. Chung, *Luther and Buddhism*, 206.
29. Ibid., 205.
30. Barth, *Church Dogmatics*, IV, 320.

viewing the embodied knowledge of Luther in his life and suffering, all are his reflection of the divine reality that he experienced through his own life. This is Luther's theology of wisdom, which Bayer names as the opposition to theology as *scientia*.

When Chung expands his perspective from a contextual theology of Korean minjung to Asian religious diversity, he shares Luther's theology of wisdom. From his experiential reality, he says the reality of God with us can embrace Asian cosmic dukkha. Luther's theology of wisdom, in which he encounters divine affirmation in his experience and history, is developed into the solidarity Christology in liberation theology. It is not a particular content of theology. Rather, it is a "disposition of doing theology from the foot of the cross." Luther's theology of wisdom can encounter the cosmic dukkha in the Asian-Buddhist context, in which suffering cannot be fully reduced to the socio-political suffering of people. Chung argues that Luther's "eucharistic presence of Jesus Christ in the Lord's Supper is the presence of the cosmic Christ who died on the cross, descended into hell, resurrected and ascended to heaven."[31] The real presence of Christ is not only for an individual sinner or for the oppressed and the poor but also for all sentient beings who live and die in cosmic dukkha.

Solidarity and Affirmation

Liberation theology considers the relationship between Christ and Christians synchronically. This point of contact is the suffering reality of the cross and the crosses. The cross is the hermeneutical key for the poor and the oppressed (Tesfai) or the "heuristic device" to challenge the conflation between knowledge and power (Solberg). Christology of the cross points to the first fruit of our eschatological hope in the midst of oppression and poverty. The unity with or participation in the life of Christ forms the reality of faith rather than simple imitation of Christ. The unity and participation in Christ as liberator can only be possible by Christ who "recapitulates" our fate. Therefore, the incarnation is the initial work of the liberator, Christ, in Irenaeus. In the case of Luther, the incarnation is the concretization of the communication of attributes. Christians participate in the work of Christ. Christ participates in the suffering of Christians. The perspective of Christ's participation is larger

---

31. Chung, *Luther and Buddhism*, 121.

than each believer's contextual participation in the life of Christ. From this point, Chung proposes his comprehensive theology of the cross: "Asian theology of the cross pursues divine suffering in personal, social, political, cosmological realms and also in other religious dimensions."[32]

Like liberation theology, Chung's cosmic Christology is not exclusive of the historical Jesus. Rather, liberation and the cosmic Christ come to realize that their understandings of Christ are rooted in the historical cross of Jesus. Chung raises the thesis of the cosmic Christ in the light of the cross: "There is no Jesus apart from the cosmic Christ as conversely there is no cosmic Christ without the suffering of the historical Jesus."[33] Jesus is foundational for the cosmic Christ because we receive the cosmic dimension of divine salvation through the life, death, and resurrection of Jesus Christ. When one loses its historicity, the cosmic Christ becomes abstract. It also loses the connection between the cross of the historical Jesus and the crosses that the masses of people experience. As Thomsen understands the event of the cross as the consequence of Jesus's life and ministry for people, the cosmic Christology cannot also underestimate the historical Jesus of life and death, including the events his followers witnessed. The cosmic Christology does not invalidate the scar of the historical cross of Jesus.

On the other hand, the cross is a mirror of the heart of God: no Jesus without the cosmic Christ. Jesus's ministry for the poor and the abyss of his suffering and death paradoxically reveal the Father's motherly pain of begetting the Son from the incarnation through the descended hell into the eschatological consummation, because of the Trinitarian affirmation of the humanity of Christ from eternity. The cross is put into perspective from the incarnation to the eschatological consummation, in the salvation history of the economic Trinity. Christian agape, which was mirrored in Jesus's life and death, meets Buddhist dukkha:

> *Dukkha* is not merely of human or all sentient beings, but of divine life.... Christian agape, which is realized in Jesus Christ's voluntarily detached renunciation from clinging to God, is not in opposition to the Buddhist concept of self-awakening to realize true self, or the *mahakaruna* (great compassion) that is a capacity of suffering with others.[34]

32. Ibid., 188.
33. Ibid., 191.
34. Ibid., 190–1.

As Thomsen argues, a theology of the cross is rooted in the historical ministry and movement rooted in Jesus's proclamation of the reign of God. Jesus is the embodiment of the metacosmic love of the Abba-God. Chung explicates the content of the heart of Abba-God in the Trinitarian theology of the cross. That is the perichoretic affirmation of the humanity of Christ from eternity. It is the cosmic, all-embracing heart of the Trinitarian God. Therefore, he calls it "Trinitarian theism." The "Father's motherly pain of begetting the Son" pervades the life, ministry, and death of Jesus. Trinitarian theism reveals the affirmation of humanity—not only the humanity of Jesus but also all human beings in Jesus's self-emptying ministry until his death. The self-manifestation of the immanent Trinity brings Christianity into discipleship, which serves the world toward the eschatological consummation because of the historical form of revelation embodied in Jesus's life and death. This mirroring relationship between the immanent and economic Trinity converges in Jesus Christ as the "mirror of the Father's heart." This heart is full of solidarity with the suffering in the world. Therefore, while Chung takes the reality of the forsaken world seriously in line with Moltmann's crucified God in Trinitarian form, he sets up a different biblical passage for Christ in the encounter of the cosmic dukkha, in which the Father, the Son, and the Spirit co-suffer with the cosmic dukkha.

Jesus's Final Word of Trust for the Abba-God.

Viewing the cross in the light of divine dukkha in the Asian context of the cosmic dukkha, Chung proposes Luke 23:46 as the foundational passage: "Father, into your hand, I commend my spirit." The absolute trust for Abba-God that Jesus showed encounters the Asian self-emptying God. Chung places the communication of attributes into the perspective of Trinity. The Trinitarian affirmation of the humanity of Christ from eternity is characteristic of the cosmic Christology of the cross. To confess that Jesus is Christ means an affirmation of salvation history through Christ's incarnation, death, descending into hell, through resurrection, and into eschatological consummation. Jesus was born and died on the cross. Luther's theology of the cross looked at the human event in Jesus in the light of the divine event in which the Trinitarian God eternally embraces the death and life of humanity. As current liberation theologians point out, the theology of the cross in the cosmic Christology can also say that the cross is nothing other than human violence, cruelty, and tragedy imposed on an innocent man. It is not redemptive in itself. In this point, the cosmic theology of the cross agrees with the "Christian mission toward abolition of the cross."[35]

The emphasis of Luther's theology of the cross is not sanctification of any violence but the divine commitment even in such a godless event. In saying so, Luther was speaking just in a descriptive way, a matter resulting from his life and experience. It is an experience that theology as scientia cannot explain, because theology as scientia cannot make divine things relate to contingent and historical events. The Trinitarian affirmation of the cosmic dukkha does not disturb us to see the death and suffering in this world in the hand of the suffering God as well as Jesus's crucifixion. Only in this way can the cosmic theology of the cross affirm divine working in the midst of cosmic dukkha. In this context, Chung says that Jesus's cry to God is not necessarily a foundational passage. Rather, Jesus's commending of his spirit to the Father is founded on "nevertheless:"

> A yes to the cross of Christ is also a yes to the cosmic Christ present outside Christianity and also a yes to the crosses of people of other faiths. Our conformity to Christ's passion expresses a trinitarian way of participating in cosmos, society and human being. The divine *dukkha* is assumed eternally and beforehand in the essential Trinity and reaches its climax in the historical incarnation and self-immolation of Jesus Christ to whom all sentient living creatures are enhypastatically-anhypostatically related, posited and exalted.[36]

Being firmly grounded in Luther's theology of the cross, Chung comes to the immense matrix of Asian religiosity: cosmic dukkha. I will finally review Chung's theology of the cross in dialogue with the other theologians I have explicated.

CONCLUDING ARGUMENTS

The Development of Trinity

Following Luther's theology of the cross, Kitamori does not stop talking about sin and the wrath of God, which are alien to Japanese religious tradition. He distinctively speaks about the absolute Other (*Zettai tasha*) who confronts sinners in the tradition of "submerged transcendence," but this God is different from the Hellenistic impassible and unchange-

---

35. This is the title of the article about the theology of the cross written by Song in *Scandal of a Crucified World*, 130–48.

36. Chung, *Luther and Buddhism*, 270.

able deity. God is pained because of the absolute Other who embraces the others (sinners). In the cross, the Son suffers the death and the Father suffers the death of the Son. The cross is the place to reveal the painful heart of God, by nature, in a Trinitarian form.

In saying that the essence of God is pain in the relationship between the Father and the Son, the incarnation of Christ means that the divinity of Christ goes outside himself. The "going outside" makes it possible to include human beings who go outside the grace of God. For Kitamori, "The pain of God is nothing but the outsideness of God's selfsameness."[37] The Son suffers by his going outside his divinity, and the Father suffers by the Son's outsidedness (alienation). He firmly grounds the pain of God in the immanent Trinity. While he barely speaks about the pain of the Son of God on the cross, pain converges in the Father's pain for letting the Son die. It is remarkable that Kitamori challenges the Hellenistic divine impassibility by focusing on Luther's theology of the cross and attempting to disclose the eternal essence of pain in the immanent Trinity. He relies on Luther's theology of the cross, by which he believes that the synthesis between love and wrath can bring something new to Japanese religious tradition.

When Chung develops Luther's theology of the cross into the perspective of divine dukkha, he puts Christ's suffering into the perichoretic divine dukkha. He argues that the divine dukkha is "expressive of the wounded heart of God eternally and beforehand for the world."[38] On this point do Kitamori and Chung share their point of view in the Asian context. However, through Chung's full development of a Trinitarian theology of the cross in the context of cosmic dukkha we come to a clear divergence between Kitamori and Chung.

First of all, Kitamori's pain of God never develops a Christology of solidarity, which has been central in the contextual theologies of the cross since liberation theology arose. Just as liberation theology criticizes the shortcomings of the development of Luther's theology of the cross in liberative perspective, because of his individual-forensic understanding of the cross, so minjung theology does it to Kitamori. On the other hand, just as North American theologians reconsider Luther in the light of orthopraxis, Chung finds the cosmic dimension of Luther beyond the

---

37. Michalson, "Theology of the Pain," 90
38. Chung, "Trinity and Asian Theology," 136.

individual-forensic feature. Following are decisive critiques that Chung gives the theology of the pain of God in the light of the cosmic Christ.

First, according to Chung, the theology of the pain of God is deeply synthesized in Luther's individual-forensic understanding of forgiveness of sin, and Kitamori develops the pain of God on the cross into the painful heart of the Father letting the Son die, but he fails to account for Luther's cosmic dimension of Christology. While this failure leads him to a disconnection with the liberative Christology in solidarity with socio-political victims, it also leads to the neglect of Asian Eucharistic theology in relation to Luther's doctrine of the real presence of Christ and the ubiquity of Christ's body. It seems to be crucial for Chung, because "a celebration of the real presence of Jesus Christ in memory and faith moves in the eschatological direction towards hope."[39] This neglect of the cosmic Christ in Luther's theology leads to the difference between Kitamori's monarchical Trinitarian theology and Chung's "Tritheism."

In line with Kitamori's contextual issue of Japanese kami tradition, he focuses on the explanation of the Christian God with a biblical image of God, which is certainly in line with Luther's theology. However, the emphasis on the monotheistic sovereign deity creates a different problem with his theology, though I keep the period of his publication in mind. This emphasis results in neglecting to address the cross in the light of both the human Jesus and the second article of the creed on Christ. As Kabuki drama is concerned about the father's feeling of letting his son die, Kitamori is concerned about disclosing the heart of the Father who lets the Son die. The cross of Jesus Christ is considered as the very means for revealing the heart of the Father. As a consequence, the pain of God loses the perichoretic communication of pain between the Father, the Son, and the Spirit and by the same token, between God and human beings. From the perspective of the cosmic Christ, it also fails to lift up the emptying Jesus to the unselfish love for others in the freedom of the Son. This entangles Kitamori with the subjugation of the cross of the Son with the brutal image of the Father who lets the Son die on the cross from eternity. In order to develop Chung's "Tritheism" in the Asian context of cosmic dukkha, it is necessary to use the logic of soku (not one, not two).

The suffering of the cross as the event within the economic Trinity is also the event in which the immanent Trinity manifests its own heart. It is along the same line as Moltmann's Trinitarian theology of the cross

39. Ibid., 136.

that comes from Luther's theology of the cross. Chung also agrees with Moltmann in that he seeks the identity between the immanent and the economic Trinity in an eschatological framework.[40] However, Chung comes to a divergent point when he develops an "Asian staurocentric Trinity:"

> The *theologia crucis,* seen in a Trinitarian way, forms a middle of time related to a metaphor of essential Trinity of mother-quality of God's giving birth as well as a metaphor of slain Lamb of the eschatological Trinity. . . . Lutheran thinking of Trinity . . . extends a threefold nondual relationship among essential, economic and eschatological trinities in which divine *dukkha* stands at the center.[41]

Going beyond the individual-forensic understanding of the cross, Chung constructs the Trinitarian theology of the cross in which the perichoretical affirmation of the humanity of Christ is self-revealed in saying that "we perceive of a motherly pain of the Father begetting the Son in the womb of the Spirit."[42] This Trinitarian metaphor is grounded in the foundational passage of Jesus's trust in the Abba-God rather than Jesus's cry of the Father's abandonment of the Son:

> The Son's kenotic emptiness is not perceived of by the Father's brutal forsakenness of the Son, but his eternal decision for realizing the cosmic unselfish love for all living creatures in the cosmic *dukkha.* This is the Great Death of the Son in the immolation of the cross.[43]

From this perspective, Chung criticizes Kitamori, as well as Luther and Moltmann, in that all take it for granted that "the Father's abandonment of the son is exemplified by the Abraham-Isaac typology."[44] The "motherly pain of the Father begetting the Son in the womb of the Spirit" is more foundational than the cross event of the Father letting the Son die. In the former, we can talk about the model of "God's giving love in sharing the death of the Son, or Father's co-suffering the death of the

---

40. Chung, *Luther and Buddhism,* 256.
41. Ibid., 257–8.
42. Chung, "Trinity and Asian Theology," 139.
43. Ibid., 142.
44. Ibid., 136.

Son."[45] Neither is identical (not one) nor inseparable (not two). Chung clearly shows the different dimensions of the divine dukkha by using the advitic logic (soku). A crucial point in comparison with Kitamori's Trinitarian theology of the cross lies in the fact that Chung distinguishes the divine dukkha in the immanent Trinity from the divine dukkha in the manifestation of the cross in the economic Trinity. The former is the "motherly pain" from eternity within the immanent Trinity (i.e., the eternal affirmation of humanity of Christ). The latter is the suffering of the Son in solidarity with victims (minjung in Chung). They are not one but not two. In addition, the latter is irreversible with the former.

Standing on the soku relationship between the suffering of the brutal death on the cross in solidarity with victims and the suffering of the eternal affirmation within the immanent Trinity, it is affirmative of Thomsen's rejection, with other liberation theologians, of the demanding Father letting the Son die, but at the same time, it remains affirmative of the divine event on the cross. If the cross event is founded on the Trinitarian affirmation of humanity from eternity, it is not dependent on divine providence but on the divine invitation to all human beings in solidarity with the poor and the oppressed in the promise of the eschatological consummation. The cross is the consequence of the risky ministry of Jesus, who engaged in a divine invitation for all. The divine suffering in the cross should be distinguished from the motherly pain of the Father begetting the Son, but both divine dukkha should not be separated until the eschatological moment of "God-with-them" (Rev 21:3). Arguing in this way, Chung comes close to Thomsen's cruciformed *missio dei*, though they have different emphases, Christ-centric or tri-centric.[46]

Chung's Trinitarian theology of the cross presents a paradigm shift from the Abraham-Isaac typology into the perichoretic co-sufferer of the Triune God. He makes it possible to encounter Christ as liberator with the cosmic Christ. In other words, his theology of the cross reaches the comprehensive understanding of the socio-political suffering and the cosmic suffering of all sentient beings, including human beings. His theology of the cross opens a new way of doing a theology of the cross in the combination between liberative Christ and cosmic Christ. His theol-

45. Chung, *Luther and Buddhism*, 340.

46. Chung proposes the *missio Trinitatis* (mission of the Trinity) in "A Theology of Justification and God's Mission," 118.

ogy of the cross points out the shortcomings of Kitamori's theology of the cross in the Asian context of suffering because of his limitation in the individual dimension. On the other hand, there remain some questions: How can the comprehensive theology of the cross speak about the individual agony of sin that Kitamori focused on? Conversely, is there something that the personal-individual realm, which Kitamori pursues, can speak to the comprehensive perception of suffering? It seems to be meaningful to review Kitamori's motif again for future conversations because he sees the personal agony of suffering from different angles than liberation theology.

Kitamori's theological motif comes from a simple, but often overlooked, reality of human love, when he says, "We feel pain only when a loved one suffers or dies."[47] It is worth remembering that Kitamori introduces Kabuki drama to explain the Father's pain for the death of the Son not in an analogical way but in an ironical way.[48] When one recognizes the analogical relation between the father's pain of sacrificing his primogeniture for his loyalty to the lord and the Father's pain of letting the Son die, Kitamori seems to bring the Kabuki drama into a theological rhetoric in an analogical way. On the other hand, he also mentions the ironic difference between them:

> The pain in Japanese tragedy, however, belongs only to the latter case [the heart of God who sacrifices his only beloved Son]. Even Japanese tragedy does not know the pain which is experienced by loving the unworthy, the unlovable, and even the enemy.[49]

This quotation helps us clearly to understand Kitamori's main motif in his theology of the cross. He enhances loving one's enemy for the view of God rather than the ethical commandment. Accepting the otherness bound to sinfulness and pain occurs in theology. The acceptance is not a simple acceptance but a painful acceptance. The cross, for him, is the symbol of the acceptance of alienation from the side of God. This is rooted in Luther's perception through the theology of the cross:

---

47. Kitamori, *Theology of the Pain*, 53.

48. I follow Westhelle's insight into "irony" for reading Luther. Westhelle considers Luther's rhetoric of irony as the "ironic deconstruction of analogy," as he says: "It is impossible to read Luther without encountering again and again the ironic moves that break up continuities and systems of correspondence, but a total surrender of analogy would lead to cynicism, even nihilism," *Scandalous God*, 44–45.

49. Ibid., 138.

> Sinners are attractive because they are loved; they are not loved because they are attractive. For this reason the love of man avoids sinners and evil persons. . . . This is love of the cross, born of the cross, which turns in the direction where it does not find good that it may enjoy, but where it may confer good upon bad and needy person.[50]

Kitamori still touches on the deep human psyche that an individual retains in ordinary life. Thus, this perception of reality seems to be a perennial issue as to how to sustain this dimension in the divided reality of human relationships even in the Asian context of the cosmic dukkha. If contextual theology seeks dialogue, mutual understanding, and communion with others by the axis of difference, not by the axis of sameness, do we still not need to maintain this insight in the face of intercontextual wholeness? One crucial question lies in how to comprehensively relate different layers of suffering. Yagi's theology, in dialogue with Buddhism, is more effective in explaining this issue.

The Development of Theology of the Cross in the Encounter with the Cosmic Dukkha

Chung believes that Buddhist realism is not irrelevant to Luther's realism of *theologia crucis*. It features three related realities: the impermanence of all things, the universality of the dukkha, and the absence of a permanent self.[51] Luther's feeling of abnegation by the wrathful God in his guilty consciousness is well explored by Yagi's analysis of egoism, which he calls the "moral and religious" egoism. In saying so, Yagi follows the Buddhist manner of liberation and starts with the recognition of the absence of the true self in the ego, and then discusses the emancipation from the empirical ego by awakening to the true self (Buddhism) and Christ as the inner other. From this perspective, it is not enough to receive the forgiveness of sin from external words in the I-Thou relationship because what is crucial is the subject itself who receives justification. As long as the "mere ego" seeks a solution, one's situation gets worse. It requires the more radical conversion within the subject, but not by human works or external work outside the subject. That is the Christ who takes place in the true self within the subject. This Christ

---

50. Luther, "Heidelberg Disputation," 57.
51. Chung, *Luther and Buddhism*, 332.

is functional, not ontological, for Yagi. It is not given by a particular point of history but has been given from the beginning. Therefore, it is a matter of awakening to Christ who makes a human being truly human. Therefore, his Buddhist Christology rejects the idea that Jesus is the first and ultimate person who accomplished contact with God. Jesus should be understood as the one who lived with the "ego awakened to the Self/Christ." Yagi's Christology is similar to Panikkar's Christology: "Jesus is the Christ, but this sentence does not mean that the Christ is Jesus. Christ can go by many historical names."[52]

Yagi understands the Chalcedonian distinction between the humanity and divinity of Jesus Christ as the actualization of the functional union between humanity and divinity in Jesus against ontological union. Christ is the field where the functional union with God takes place, and at the same time, the action of God within the subject. True humanity and true divinity simultaneously take place in the ego awakened to the Self/Christ. The concentration on the liberation from the individual ego in the cosmic dukkha (the impermanency of all sentient beings) can well be connected with Luther's idea of "wonderful exchange" (happy exchange) because this idea implies "a concept of the unitive marriage between the sinful empirical ego and the true self of Christ."[53] This is a universal fact, but this is an actualization that must take place in the individual person. Thus, Yagi, as well as Abe, seeks a solution in terms of the cosmic dukkha in "cosmo-existentialism." As a consequence, he deals with the cross as a mere symbol. It is difficult to find in Yagi's theology the dynamic relationship between Jesus's life and death and our embodied suffering. While Jesus is the one awakened to the true self for Yagi, Luther's "wonderful exchange" is firmly based on the historical event of the cross of Jesus. It becomes clear that Buddhist Christology in Yagi takes a different way from Luther's Christology in the light of the cross of Jesus when Chung summarizes:

> The encounter with the self here immediately opens up an encounter with the God who is utterly other and the creator of the finite self. However, the Buddhist intuition of self does not work this way, but opens onto the *Sunyata* as the Great Self.[54]

---

52. Ibid., 327. See also Panikkar, *Unknown Christ of Hinduism*, 48–49.
53. Chung, *Luther and Buddhism*, 334.
54. Ibid., 335.

Chung develops the cosmic eschatological hope by going beyond the individual awakening event in terms of self-emptying. The cross of Jesus is the mirror of the motherly pain of God begetting the Son in the power of the Spirit. The backside of this cosmic theology of the cross is the liberative theology of the cross and vice versa. If it is correct to insist on this compatibility, we have to ask one more time the epistemic key that Westhelle proposes in the Asian context.

The Epistemic Key in the Cosmic Christ of the Cross

The epistemic key raises the question "why" in terms of the historical cross of Jesus. This question includes an answer. Jesus was crucified because he asked, "Why?" Westhelle considers Jesus's ministry as Foucault's "*parrhesis*" (to speak the truth boldly) and Gandhi's "*satyagraha*" (truth-force). The cross provides a powerful symbol to speak about Great Death and Great Life in Zen tradition. This cross points to spiritual death. The epistemic key does not exclude the use of the cross in that way, but it always urges us not to forget the fact that the cross is Jesus's cross. The historical cross of Jesus is the embodiment of suffering and death of Jesus, who boldly spoke for those who suffered from abnegation by law. The existential hermeneutics, which influences Yagi's theology, reduces or excludes some parts of the narrative of the cross and resurrection when they cannot be taken in their own existential meanings. He interprets the resurrection as demythologizing meaning for contemporary people, in which he shares that there are some stories in Buddhism in which the holy person was raised from death.[55]

It is important to Yagi to find common religious experience between Jesus, Buddha and current "us." Atonement theories are rejected if grounded on the historical Jesus and his cross as if it attained the fundamental change between God and human beings in terms of the "primordial fact." Conversely, there is no room to ask about the epistemic key. The perspective of the epistemic key is not reduced to the meaning of interpreter. It remains the "thorn of history." The key is to bring the simple form of "why?" Jesus calls suffering what it is. The cross speaks about Jesus as he is. Jesus did not die simply when he grew old. It is right to say that Jesus was killed by human cruelty or political power. But why? It is because Jesus's life and ministry confronted them. Still, I

---

55. Yagi, "What Can Claim Absoluteness?" 39–41.

have to ask, why? It is because he was awakened to Christ in him as the functional union with God. Thomsen calls it "Jesus-spirituality." They seem to share the common ground on this level.

However, the epistemic key creates a watershed between them when it makes us pay attention to the simple fact that Jesus was not merely an awakened person. Jesus lived in the "reign of Abba-God" (Thomsen) and was "awakened to the Self/Christ" (Yagi) and was refused by the world. The cross was an event in which the dominant social, political, and religious order killed him by order of the Roman Empire. They did not tolerate his ministry and life. They killed him. This key overlaps with the questions some feminist/womanist theologians bring into a theology of the cross that put a redemptive meaning into the brutal death.[56] C. S. Song also argues an Asian missiology toward abolishing the cross for the same reason.

The cross shed light on the condition of this world. Nevertheless, the cosmic Christ in the light of the cross does not invalidate the question why. Who is the Abba to whom Jesus commended himself? Following Luther's phrase, "Jesus is the mirror of the Father," Chung clarifies the heart of God in a Trinitarian form: the pain of God begetting the Son in the power of the Holy Spirit. The cosmic Christ, which paradoxically appeared on the cross, maintains its own question in holding the epistemic key. In the moment of absence, intransitive faith worked through the power of Holy Spirit. This theology of the cross is not aimed at insisting on the metaphysical ground of salvation. Rather, it clarifies the historical contact with divine affirmation of all sentient beings through the abyss of the cross of Jesus and through the historical interpretation of his followers. Therefore, it requires discipleship of the cross.

Cosmic Christ in Global Context

I explained in chapter 1 that Thomsen's cruciformed *missio dei* sustains the normativity of Jesus's ministry of the reign of God in the context of global missiology:

> Only when the power of creative, life-transforming, persistent, persevering and vulnerable love, embodied in the crucified Jesus, becomes normative for the Christian community's proclamation and

---

56. For a detailed discussion of this matter, see Brock and Parker, *Proverbs of Ashes*; Williams, "Black Women's Surrogacy Experience," 19–32; Terrell, "Our Mothers' Gardens," 33–49.

praxis will the church begin to be a transforming agent within the human community and a dialogical partner with the full human family. Only then will the Jesus movement authentically proclaim the life-transforming power of Christ as the crucified Truth.[57]

What Jesus's ministry brought is the metacosmic love of Abba-God. Only in this meaning does Thomsen recognize the normativity of Jesus. Thomsen is affirmative of Aulen's proposal about Luther's connection to the classical atonement theory. However, unlike Aulen, Thomsen does not consider the cosmic dimension of Luther's theology of the cross within the framework of atonement theory but in the framework of the participation in Jesus's movement of the actualization of the reign of God. The cosmic Christ for Thomsen is embodied in Jesus's life and death, and by the same token, in those who live with others looking for the eschatological hope grounded on the metacosmic love of the Abba-God. Unlike Aulen, he understands the battleground with evil powers that Irenaeus depicts as not merely ancient myth that should be demythologized but as a metaphor that points to the reality of the world in mythical form. The mythical form is the reality of the broken world and the depth of the darkness to the extent that Jesus was killed and by the same token, many innocents were cast away and are still being broken.

The cross is not a symbol for spiritual death. The cross is also not the myth to provide something meaningful. Rather, it awakens those who think that it is myth to the fact that it is the historical reality in which they lived and we live. The cross is the consequence of Jesus's commitment to the reign of God for people, not the consequence of his awakening to the true Self/Christ in his own spiritual awakening. Accordingly, unlike any atonement theories, "Jesus was not sent to die: he came to live and challenge Satan and all his powers."[58] The resurrection means nothing other than the resurrection of the crucified: "the resurrection is the sign of hope in the midst of a raging battle that God ultimately will have God's will done."[59] Therefore, a cruciformed missiology is in line with the cosmic Christology that is rooted in Irenaeus. It takes its perspective within the eschatological consummation. In the face of religious dialogue, the cruciformed *missio dei* is grounded in a radical inclusivism. The ground of Christianity lies in the cruciformed *missio dei* embodied

---

57. Thomsen, *Christ Crucified*, 76.
58. Ibid., 26.
59. Ibid., 26.

in Jesus's ministry and cross. It maintains a theologian of the cross for the poor and the oppressed, who are not merely an epistemological priority without the elements of *agape* Christianity. Jesus embodied the love of God for suffering people. It seems to Abe that the ultimate is mixed up with the penultimate. However, this penultimate is "con-fused" (Keller) as much as we cannot break from the ultimate. Chung finds the other Buddhist tradition in this perspective.

Chung finds the constructive perception of the cosmic dukkha in Tich Nacht Hanh, not in the absolute Nothingness. Tich Nacht Hanh, who engages in the social justice movement in Buddhism, says, "Wealth is made of non-wealth elements, and poverty is made by non-poverty elements."[60] This constructive insight of an inter-penetrating and the inter-dependence of society is true of the inter-penetrating and inter-dependent reality of human existence. The reason we stand by the poor and the oppressed is not a matter of charity but the consequence of awakening to our own dependency upon others. Following this line, Chung shows his ethical concern:

> Emancipation comes from the transformation of the poor people's consciousness by penetrating into the nature of inter-being. Through this transformation, the poor will know that they bear the pain of the whole world. This is the principle of interpenetration, which reveals that everything contains everything else.[61]

The love of God for the poor and the oppressed is the other side of the divine affirmation of the world's creatures in the midst of the cosmic dukkha. Jesus is the awakened one who proclaimed and practiced the reign of God who never gives up on the abnegated and cries from the depth of sin, death, and evil until the eschatological consummation. The cross is a contingent event—that is correct. But the theology of the cross affirms that divine cosmic love works though this contingent existence in the cosmic world, in which nothing is isolated from the Other/others.

---

60. Chung, *Luther and Buddhism*, 341.
61. Ibid., 135.

Bibliography

Abe, Masao. "Faith and Self-Awakening: A Search for the Fundamental Category Covering All Religious Life." *Eastern Buddhist* 31/1 (1998) 12–24.
———. "Kenotic God and Dynamic Sunyata." In *The Emptying God: A Buddhist-Jewish-Christian Conversation*, edited by John B. Cobb Jr. and Christopher Ives. Maryknoll, NY: Orbis, 1990.
———. "A Rejoinder." In *The Emptying God: A Buddhist-Jewish-Christian Conversation*, edited by John B. Cobb Jr. and Christopher Ives, 3–68. Maryknoll, NY: Orbis, 1990.
———. "Suffering in the Light of Our Time: Our Time in the Light of Suffering: Buddha's First Holy Truth." In *Buddhism and Interfaith Dialogue*, edited by Steven Heine, 73–85. Honolulu: University of Hawaii Press, 1995.
———. *Zen and Western Thought*. Edited by Wilham R. LaFleur. Honolulu: University of Hawaii Press, 1985.
Abe, Masao, and Paul F. Knitter. "Spirituality and Liberation: A Buddhist-Christian Conversation." In *Buddhism and Interfaith Dialogue*, edited by Steven Heine, 223–43. Honolulu: University of Hawaii Press, 1995.
Ahn, Byung-Mu, "Jesus and *Ochlos* in the Context of His Galilean Ministry." In *Asian Contextual Theology for the Third Millennium: Theology of Minjung in Fourth-Eye Formation*, edited by Paul S.Chung, Veli-Matti Karkkainen, and Kim Kyoung-Jae, 33–50. Eugene, OR: Wipf & Stock, 2007.
Akutagawa, Ryunosuke. "The Faint Smiles of the Gods." In *The Essential Akutagawa*, edited by Seiji M. Lippit, 115–28. New York: Marsilio, 1999.
Althaus, Paul. *The Theology of Martin Luther*. Translated by Robert C. Schultz. Philadelphia: Fortress, 1966.
Altizer, Thomas. "Buddhist Emptiness and the Crucifixion of God." In *The Emptying God: A Buddhist-Jewish-Christian Conversation*, edited by John B. Cobb Jr. and Christopher Ives, 69–78. Maryknoll, NY: Orbis, 1990.
Altmann, Walter. *Luther and Liberation: A Latin American Perspective*. Minneapolis: Fortress, 1992.
Ariarajah, S. Wesley. "Intercultural Hermeneutics: A Promise for the Future." *Exchange* 34/2 (2005) 89–101.
Aulén, Gustaf. *Christus Victor: An Historical Study of The Three Main Types of the Idea of Atonement*. Eugene, OR: Wipf & Stock, 2003.
Barth, Karl. *Church Dogmatics*. IV. Edited by G. W. Bromiley and T. F. Torrance. Edinburgh, Scotland: T & T. Clark, 1958.
———. Preface to *Fukuinshugi shingaku nyumon* (*Introduction to Evangelical Theology*). Translated by Tsuneaki Kato. Tokyo: Shinkyo shuppansha, 1962.
Bayer, Oswald. *Theology the Lutheran Way*. Edited and translated by Jeffrey G. Silcock and Mark C. Mattes. Grand Rapids: Eerdmans, 2007.

Bellah, Robert N. *Imaging Japan: The Japanese Tradition and Its Modern Interpretation.* Los Angeles: University of California Press, 2003.

———. *Tokugawa Religion: The Cultural Roots of Modern Japan.* New York: The Free Press, 1957; 1985.

Bergmann, Sigurd. *God in Context: A Survey of Contextual Theology.* Burlington, VT: Ashgate, 2003.

Bevans, Stephen B. *Models of Contextual Theology: Revised and Expanded Edition.* Maryknoll, NY: Orbis, 2005.

Bevans, Stephen B., and Roger P. Schroeder. *Constants in Context: A Theology of Mission for Today.* Maryknoll, NY: Orbis, 2004.

Bosch, David J. *Transforming Mission: Paradigm Shifts in Theology of Mission.* Maryknoll, NY: Orbis, 1991.

Bowker, John. *Problems of Suffering in Religions of the World.* London: Cambridge University Press, 1975.

Brock, Rita Nakashima, and Rebecca Ann Parker. *Proverbs of Ashes: Violence, Redemptive Suffering and the Search for What Saves Us.* Boston: Beacon, 2001.

Bussie, Jacqeline A. *The Laughter of the Oppressed: Ethical and Theological Resistance in Wiesel, Morrison, and End.* New York: T & T Clark, 2007.

Chappell, David. "Introduction to Divine Emptiness and Historical Fullness." In *Divine Emptiness and Historical Fullness: A Buddhist Jewish Christian Conversation with Masao Abe,* edited by Christopher Ives, ix–xiii. Valley Forge, PA: Trinity, 1995.

Choi, Jung-Bong. "Mapping Japanese Imperialism onto Postcolonial Criticism." *Social Identities* 9/3 (2003) 325–40.

Chung, Paul. *Christian Mission and a Diakonia of Reconciliation: A Global Reframing of Justification and Justice.* Minneapolis: Lutheran University Press, 2008.

———. "Dietrich Bonhoeffer Seen from Asian Minjung Theology and the Fourth Eye of Socially Engaged Buddhism." In *Asian Contextual Theology for the Third Millennium: Theology of Minjung in Fourth-Eye Formation,* edited by Paul S. Chung, Veli-Matti Karkkainen, and Kim Kyoung-Jae, 127–46. Eugene, OR: Wipf & Stock, 2007.

———. "Discovering the Relevance of Martin Luther for Asian Theology." *Dialogue: A Journal of Theology* 44/1 (2005) 38–49.

———. "The Future of Martin Luther in an Asian Context." *Dialogue: A Journal of Theology* 42/1 (2003) 62–74.

———. Introduction of *Asian Contextual Theology for the Third Millennium: Theology of Minjung in Fourth-Eye Formation,* edited by Paul S, Chung, Veli-Matti Karkkainen, and Kim Kyoung-Jae, 1–14. Eugene, OR: Wipf & Stock, 2007.

———. *Karl Barth: God's Word in Action.* Eugene, OR: Cascade Books, 2008.

———. "Lutheran Theology in Engagement with World Religions." *Dialog: A Journal of Theology* 46/4 (2007) 335–43.

———. *Martin Luther and Buddhism: Aesthetics of Suffering.* Eugene, OR: Wipf & Stock, 2002.

———. "Martin Luther and Shinran: The Presence of Christ in Justification and Salvation in a Buddhist-Christian Context." *Asia Journal of Theology* 18/2 (2004) 295–309.

———. "Mission and Inculturation in the Thought of Matteo Ricci." In *Asian Contextual Theology for the Third Millennium: Theology of Minjung in Fourth-Eye Formation,* edited by Paul S. Chung, Veli-Matti Karkkainen, and Kim Kyoung-Jae, 303–28. Eugene, OR: Wipf & Stock, 2007.

———. "The Mystery of God and *Tao* in Jewish-Christian-Taoist Context." In *Asian Contextual Theology for the Third Millennium: Theology of Minjung in Fourth-Eye Formation*, edited by Paul S. Chung, Veli-Matti Karkkainen, and Kim Kyoung-Jae, 243–66. Eugene, OR: Wipf & Stock, 2007.

———. "A Theology of Justification and God's Mission." *Currents in Theology and Mission* 34/2 (2007) 117–27.

———. "Trinity and Asian Theology of Divine Dukkar." *Asia Journal of Theology* 16/1 (2002) 131–47.

Cobb, John B. Jr. "On the Deepening of Buddhism." In *The Emptying God: A Buddhist-Jewish-Christian Conversation*, edited by John B. Cobb Jr. and Christopher Ives, 91–101. Maryknoll, NY: Orbis, 1990.

Cobb, John B. Jr. and Christopher Ives, editors. *The Emptying God: A Buddhist-Jewish-Christian Conversation*. Maryknoll, NY: Orbis, 1990.

Cone, James H. *A Black Theology of Liberation*. Philadelphia: Lippincott, 1970.

———. *God of the Oppressed*, revised edition. Maryknoll, NY: Orbis, 1997.

Drummond, Richard Henry. "A Giant in Biblical Studies from the Far East." *Journal of Ecumenical Studies* 40/3 (2003).

Eager, Max. "Modernization and Secularization in Japan: A Polemical Essay." *Japanese Journal of Religious Studies* 7/1 (1980) 7–24.

Ebeling, Gerhard. *Luther: An Introduction to His Thought*. Translated by R. A. Wilson. London: Collins, 1970.

Endo, Shusaku. *Deep River*. Translated by Van C. Gessel. New York: New Directions, 1994.

———. *The Sea and Poison*. Translated by Michael Gallagher. London: Owen, 1972.

———. *Silence*. Translated by William Johnston. New York: Taplinger, 1980; Monumenta Nipponica, 1969.

Endo, Shusaku, and Van C. Gessel, editors. *"Endo Shusaku" To Shusaku Endo: Amerika "Chinmoku to Koe": Endo Bungaku Kenkyu Hokoku* (*Endo Shusaku and Shasaku Endo: Silence and Voice in America: the Report of the Association of the Study of Endo Literature*). Tokyo: Shunjusha, 1994.

Forde, Gerhard O. *On Being a Theologian of the Cross: Reflections on Luther's Heidelberg Disputation, 1518*. Grand Rapids: Eerdmans, 1997.

———. "The Work of Christ." In *Christian Dogmatics* vol. 2, edited by Robert W. Jenson, 5–99. Philadelphia: Fortress, 1984.

Fritsch-Oppermann, Sybille C. "Christian Existence in a Buddhist Context: The Theology of Yagi as a Contribution to an Interreligious Hermeutics of the 'Other.'" *Studies in Interreligious Dialogue* 13/2 (2003) 215–39.

Furuya, Yasuo, editor. *A History of Japanese Theology*. Grand Rapids: Eerdmans, 1997.

González, Justo L. *Christian Thought Revisited: Three Types of Theology*. Maryknoll, NY: Orbis, 1999.

Gutierrez A., Gustavo. *Theology of Liberation: History, Politics, and Salvation*. Edited and translated by Caridad Inda and John Eagleson. Maryknoll, NY: Orbis, 1973.

Hall, Douglas J. *The Cross in Our Context: Jesus and the Suffering World*. Minneapolis: Fortress, 2003.

———. *God and Human Suffering of the Innocent*. Maryknoll, NY: Orbis, 1987.

Harding, Sandra. *Whose Science? Whose Knowledge? Thinking from Women's Lives*. New York: Cornell University Press, 1991.

Hayashi, Makoto. "Nihon Shukyo-Shi Ni Okeru Sezokuka Katei (The Process of Secularization in the History of Japanese religion)." In *Gendai Shukyo-Gaku (The Contemporary Study of Religion)*, 4, edited by Keiichi Yanagawa, 31–57. Tokyo: Tokyo Daigaku Shuppankai, 1992.

Hendel, Kurt. "Theology of the Cross." *Current in Theology and Mission* 24/3 (1997) 223–31.

Hoekema, Alle G. "The 'Christology' of the Japanese Novelist Shusaku Endo." *Exchange* 29/3 (2000) 230–48.

Inagaki, Hisakazu and J. Nelson Jennings. *Philosophical Theology and East-West Dialogue*. Atlanta: Rodopi B. V., 2000.

Ives, Christopher, editor. *Divine Emptiness and Historical Fullness: A Buddhist Jewish Christian Conversation with Masao Abe*. Valley Forge, PA: Trinity, 1995.

Karatani, Kojin. "Uses of Aesthetics: After Orientalism." *Boundary* 25/2 (1998) 145–60.

Kasahara, Yoshimitsu. "Confession of War Responsibility, Japan." In *A Dictionary of Asian Christianity*, edited by Scott W. Sunquist, 208. Grand Rapids: Eerdmans, 2001.

Kee, Howard Clark. "The Conversion of Paul: Confrontation or Interiority." In *The Other Side of God: A Polarity in World Religions*, edited by Peter L. Berger, 48–60. Garden City, New York: Anchor, 1981.

Keller, Catherine. "More on Feminism, Self-Sacrifice, and Time; or, Too Many Words for Emptiness." *Buddhist-Christian Studies* 13 (1993) 211–19.

———. "Scoop up the Water and the Moon is in Your Hands." In *The Emptying God: A Buddhist-Jewish-Christian Conversation*, edited by John B. Cobb Jr. and Christopher Ives. Maryknoll, NY: Orbis, 1990.

Keuss, Jeff. "The Lenten Face of Christ in Shusaku Endo's Silence and Life of Jesus." *Expository Times* 118/6 (2007) 273–79.

Kim, Kirsteen. "Missiology as Global Conversation of (Contextual) Theologies." *Mission Studies* 21/1 (2004): 39–53.

Kim, Kyoung-Jae. "Christianity and Culture: A Hermeneutic of Mission Theology in an East Asian Context." In *Asian Contextual Theology for the Third Millennium: Theology of Minjung in Fourth-Eye Formation*, edited by Paul S. Chung, Veli-Matti Karkkainen, and Kim Kyoung-Jae, 147–63. Eugene, OR: Wipf & Stock, 2007.

Kim, Tae-Chang. "*A Koukyou Shukyo Shiron* (An Essay for Public Religion)." In *Koukyou-Tetsuagaku (Publish Philosophy)* 16, *Shukyo kara kangaeru kokyo-sei (Publicness from the Perspective of Religion)*, edited by Hisakazu Inagaki and Tae-Chang Kim, 107–34. Tokyo: Tokyo daigaku shuppansh, 2006.

Kitamori, Kazoh. "Christianity and Other Religions in Japan." *The Japan Christian Quarterly* 50/1 (1984) 23–30.

———. "Is 'Japanese Theology' Possible?" *The North East Asia Journal of Theology* (September 1969) 76–87.

———. *Kon-nichi no shingaku (Contemporary Theology)*. Tokyo: Nihon-no-Bara, 1984.

———. "The Problem of Pain in Christology." In *Christ and the Younger Churches*, edited by Georg F. Vicedom, 84–85. London: SPCK, 1972.

———. *Shingaku teki jiden I (Theological Autobiography I)*. Tokyo: Kyoubun kan, 1960.

———. *Shukyou kaikaku no shingaku (Theology of the Reformation)*. Tokyo: Shinkyo-Publisher, 1960.

———. *Theology of the Pain of God*. Eugene, OR: Wipf & Stock, 2005.

———. *Urei naki kami* (God without Sorrow). Tokyo: Kodansh, 1991.

Knitter, Paul F. *Jesus and the Other Names*. Maryknoll, NY: Orbis, 1997.
Kolb, Robert. "Luther on the Theology of the Cross." *Lutheran Quarterly* 16 (2002) 443–66.
Koyama, Kosuke. "The Crucified Christ Challenges Human Power." In *Asian Faces of Jesus*, edited by R. S. Sugirtharajah, 149–62. New York: Orbis, 1993.
———. *Mount Fuji and Mount Sinai: A Critique Idols*. Maryknoll, NY: Orbis, 1985.
———. *No Handle on the Cross: An Asian Meditation on the Crucified Mind*. Maryknoll, NY: Orbis, 1976.
———. "Reformation in the Global Context: The Disturbing Spaciousness of Jesus Christ." *Currents in Theology and Mission* 30/2 (2003) 119–28.
———. "Terror and Japan's Colonization of Korea 1910–1945." In *Surviving Terror: Hope and Justice in a World of Violence*, edited by Victoria Lee Erickson and Michelle Lim Jones, chapter 2. Grand Rapids: Brazos, 2002.
———. *Water Buffalo Theology: Twenty-Fifth Anniversary Edition Revised and Expandeditor*. Maryknoll, NY: Orbis, 1999.
Küng, Hans. "God's Self-Renunciation and Buddhist Emptiness: A Christian Response to Masao Abe." In. *Divine Emptiness and Historical Fullness: A Buddhist Jewish Christian Conversation with Masao Abe*, edited by Christopher Ives. Valley Forge, PA: Trinity, 1995.
Kuramatsu, Isao. "Historical Significance of *Theology of the Pain of God*." In afterword to *Kami-no Itami-no Shingaku (Theology of the Pain of God)*. Tokyo: Kodansha, 1986.
Küster, Volker. *The Many Faces of Jesus Christ: Intercultural Christology*. New York: Orbis, 2001.
———. "The Project of an Intercultural Theology." *Swedish Missiological Themes* 93/3 (2005) 417–32.
Kyung, Chung Hyun. *Struggle to Be the Sun Again: Introducing Asian Women's Theology*. Maryknoll, NY: Orbis, 1990.
Lee, Jung Young. *God Suffers for Us: A Systematic Inquiry into a Concept of Divine Passibility*. Netherlands: Martinus Nijhoff, 1974.
Lefebure, Leo D. "Awakening and Grace: Religious Identity in the Thought of Masao Abe and Karl Rahner." *Cross Current* 47/4 (1997–1998) 451–72.
———. *The Buddha & The Christ: Exploration in Buddhist and Christian Dialogue*. Maryknoll, NY: Orbis, 1993.
Loewenich, Walther V. *Luther's Theology of the Cross*. Translated by Herbert J. A. Bouman. Minneapolis: Augsburg, 1976.
Lohse, Bernhard. *Martin Luther: An Introduction to His Life and Work*. Translated by Robert C. Schults. Philadelphia: Fortress, 1986.
Luther, Martin. "Confession Concerning Christ's Supper." *Luther's Works* vol. 37, *Word and Sacrament*, edited by Robert H. Fischer. Philadelphia: Muhlenberg, 1961.
———. "Heidelberg Disputation (1518)." *Luther's Works* vol. 31, *Career of the Reformer I*, edited and translated by Harold J. Grimm. Philadelphia: Fortress, 1957.
———. "Lectures on Isaiah: Chapters 40–66." *Luther's Works* vol. 17, edited by Hilton C. Oswald. St. Louis: Concordia, 1972.
———. "Operationes in Psalmos (1519–1521)." *Dr. Martin Luthers Werke: Kritische Gesamtausgabe* vol. 5. Weimar: H. Böhlau, 1892.
———. "Preface to the Acts of the Apostles." *Luther's Works* vol. 35, *Word and Sacrament*, edited by F. Theodore Bachmann. Philadelphia: Muhlenberg, 1960.

———. "The Sacrament—Against the Fanatics." *Luther's Works* vol. 36, *Word and Sacrament*. Edited by Abdel Ross. Philadelphia: Muhlenberg, 1959.

Luz, Ulrich, and Axel Michaels. *Encountering Jesus & Buddha: Their Lives and Teaching*. Translated by Linda M. Maloney. Minneapolis: Fortress, 2006.

Madsen, Anna M. *The Theology of the Cross in Historical Perspective*. Eugene, OR: Wipf & Stock, 2007.

Mase-Hasegawa, Emi. *Christ in Japanese Culture: Theological Themes in Shusaku Endo's Literary Works*. Boston: Brill, 2008.

———. "Image of Christ for Japanese: Reflections on Shusaku Endo's Novels." *Inter-Religious Study* 43 (2003) 22–38.

Matsuoka, Fumitaka. "The Church in the World: The Christology of Shusaku Endo." *Theology Today* 39/3 (1982) 294–99.

McGrath, Alister. *Luther's Theology of the Cross: Martin Luther's Theological Breakthrough*. Cambridge: Blackwell, 1985.

McWilliams, Warren. "The Pain of God in the Theology of Kazoh Kitamori." *Perspectives in Religious Studies* 8/3 (1981) 184–200.

Meyer, Richard. "Toward a Japanese Theology: Kitamori's Theology of the Pain of God." *Concordia Theological Monthly* 33/5 (1962) 261–72.

Michalson, Carl. "The Theology of the Pain of God." In *Japanese Contribution to Christian Theology*, edited by Carl Michalson. Philadelphia: Westminster, 1960

Migliore, Daniel L. *Faith Seeking Understanding: An Introduction to Christian Theology*, 2nd edition. Grand Rapids: Eerdmans, 2004.

Miyamoto, Takeshi. *Kami no itami no shingaku wo yomu* (*Reading Theology of the Pain of God*). Tokyo: Kirisuto kyo shuppansh, 1993.

Miyoshi, Masao. *Off Center: Power & Culture Relations Between Japan and the United States*. Cambridge: Harvard University Press, 1994.

Moltmann, Jürgen. *The Crucified God: the Cross of Christ as the Foundation and Criticism of Christian Theology*. Translated by R. A. Wilson and John Bowden. Minneapolis: Fortress, 1993.

———. "God is Unselfish Love." In *The Emptying God: A Buddhist-Jewish-Christian Conversation*, edited by John B. Cobb Jr. and Christopher Ives, 116–24. Maryknoll, NY: Orbis, 1990.

Morimoto, Anri. *Ajia shingaku kougi* (*Lecture on Asian Theology*). Tokyo: Soubun-sha, 2004.

———. "The (More or Less) Same Light but from Different Lamps: The Post-Pluralist Understanding of Religion from a Japanese Perspective." *International Journal for Philosophy of Religion* 53 (2003) 163–80.

Mullins, Mark R. *Christianity Made in Japan: A Study of Indigenous Movements*. Honolulu: University of Hawaii Press, 1998.

Nausner, Michael "Homeland as Borderland: Territories of Christian Subjectivity." In *Postcolonial Theologies: Divinity and Empire*, edited by Catherine Keller, Michael Nausner, and Mayra Rivera, 118–32. St. Louis: Chalice, 2004.

Oberman, Heiko A. *Luther: Man between God and the Devil*. Translated by Eileen Walliser-Schwarzbart. New York: Doubleday, 1992.

Onodera, Isao. *Zettaimu to Kami: Kyoto-gakuha no tetsugaku* (*The Absolute Nothingness and God: The Philosophy of Kyoto-School*). Yokohama, Japan: Shunpu sha, 2002.

Ott, Heinrich. "The Convergence: Sunyata as a Dynamic Event." In *Divine Emptiness and Historical Fullness: A Buddhist Jewish Christian Conversation with Masao Abe*, edited by Christopher Ives. Valley Forge, PA: Trinity, 1995.

Otto, Randall E. "Japanese Religion in Kazoh Kitamori's *Theology of the Pain of God.*" *Encounter* 52/1 (1991) 38–48.

Panikkar, Raimundo. "The Jordan, the Tiber, and the Ganges." In *The Myth of Christian Uniqueness: Toward a Pluralistic Theology of Religions*, edited by John Hick and Paul F. Knitter, 89–116. Maryknoll, NY: Orbis, 1987.

———. *The Unknown Christ of Hinduism.* Maryknoll, NY: Orbis, 1964.

Pannenberg, Wolfhart. *Jesus—God and Man*, 2nd edition. Translated Lewis L. Wilkings and Duane A. Priebe. Philadelphia: Westminster, 1976.

Park, Andrew S. *The Wounded Heat of God: The Asian Concept of Han and the Christian Doctrine of Sin.* Nashville: Abingdon, 1993.

Pelikan, Jaroslav. *The Christian Tradition: A History of the Development of Doctrine*, vol. 1, *The Emergence of the Catholic Tradition (100–600)*. Chicago: The University of Chicago Press, 1971.

———. *The Christian Tradition: A History of the Development of Doctrine*, vol. 4, *Reformation of Church and Dogma (1300–1700)*. Chicago: The University of Chicago Press, 1984.

Pieris, Aloysius, SJ. "The Buddha and the Christ: Mediators of Liberation." In *The Myth of Christian Uniqueness: Toward A Pluralistic Theology of Religions*, edited by John Hick and Paul F. Knitter, 162–77. Maryknoll, NY: Orbis, 1987.

———. *An Asian Theology of Liberation.* Maryknoll, NY: Orbis, 1988.

Pinnington, Adrian. "Yoshimitsu, Benedict, Endo: Guilt, Shame and the Post-war Idea of Japan." *Japan Forum* 13/1 (2001) 91–105.

Piryno, Ernest D. "Japanese Theology and Inculturation." *Journal of Ecumenical Studies* 24/4 (1987) 535–56.

Prenter, Regin, *Luther's Theology of the Cross.* Philadelphia: Fortress, 1971.

Raj, Victor. "The Pain of God as the Mission of God." *Missio Apostolica* 7/1 (2004) 24–30.

Rajashekar, Paul. *Theology in Dialogue: Theology in the Context of Religious and Cultural Plurality in Asia.* Geneva, Switzerland: LWF, DCC, and DS, 1987.

Ruge-Johnes, Philip. *Cross in Tensions: Luther's Theology of the Cross as Theologico-social Critique.* Eugene, OR: Pickwick Publications, 2008.

Schreiter, Robert J. *Constructing Local Theologies.* Maryknoll, NY: Orbis, 1985.

———. "Communication and Interpretation Across Cultures: Problems and Prospects." *International Review of Mission* 85, (1996) 227–39.

———. "The Legacy of St. Francis Xavier: Inculturation of the Gospel Then and Now." *East Asian Pastoral Review* 44 (2007).

———. *The New Catholicity: Theology between the Global and the Local.* Maryknoll, NY: Orbis, 1997.

Schweitzer, Albert. *The Mysticism of Paul the Apostle.* Translated by William Montgomery. New York: Macmillan, 1955.

Segundo, Juan Luis. *The Liberation of Theology.* Translated by John Drury. Eugene, OR: Wipf & Stock, 2002.

Shore, Jeff. "Abe Masao's Legacy: Awakening to Reality through the Death of Ego and Providing Spiritual Ground for the Modern World." *The Eastern Buddhist* 31/2 (1998) 295–307.

Sittler, Joseph A. "Called to Unity." *The Ecumenical Review* 14. October–December 1961.

Sobrino, Jon. *Jesus The Liberator: A Historical-Theological View*. Maryknoll, NY: Orbis, 2004.

Solberg, Mary. *Compelling Knowledge: A Feminist Proposal for an Epistemology of the Cross*. Albany, NY: State University of New York Press, 1997.

———. "Notes Toward an Epistemology of the Cross." *Currents in Theology and Mission* 24/1 (1997) 14–22.

———. "What an Epistemology of the Cross Is Good For." In *Cross Examinations: Readings on the Meaning of the Cross Today*, edited by Marit Trelstad, 139–53. Minneapolis: Augsburg, 2006.

Song, C. S. *Jesus, the Crucified People*. Minneapolis: Fortress, 1996.

———. *Theology from the Womb of Asia*. Maryknoll, NY: Orbis, 1986.

———. *Third-eye Theology: Theology in Formation in Asian Setting*. Eugene, OR: Wipf & Stock, 2002.

Steiger, Johann Anselm. "The Communication Idiomatum as the Axle and Motor of Luther's Theology." *Lutheran Quarterly* 14 (2000) 125–58.

Sundermeier, Theo. *Das Kreuz als Befreiung*. München: Kraiser Traktate, 1985.

Suzuki, Norihisa. "On the Translation of God: Part One." *Japanese Religions* vol. 26/2 (2001) 131–46.

———. "On the Translation of God: Part Two." *Japanese Religions* vol. 27/2 (2002) 133–58.

Takizawa, Katsumi. "On *Theology of the Pain of God*." In *Shukyo wo Tou (Reflecting upon Religion)*. Tokyo: Sanitsu shobo, 1977.

Terrell, Joanne Marie. "Our Mothers' Gardens." In *Cross Examinations: Readings on the Meaning of the Cross Today*, edited by Marit Trelstad, 33–49. Minneapolis: Fortress, 2006.

Tesfai, Yacob, editor. *The Scandal of a Crucified World: Perspective on the Cross and Suffering*. New York: Orbis, 1994.

Theological Education Fund. *Ministry in Context: The Third Mandate Programme of the Theological Education Fund (1970–1977)*. Bromley, Kent: New Life, 1972.

Thomas, M. M., "A Christ-centered Humanist Approach to Religions in the Indian Pluralistic Context." In *Christian Uniqueness Reconsidered*, edited by D'Costa, 49–62. Maryknoll, NY: Orbis, 1987.

Thompson, Deanna A. *Crossing the Divide: Luther, Feminism, and the Cross*. Minneapolis: Fortress, 2004.

Thomsen, Mark. *Christ Crucified: A 21st-century Missiology of the Cross*. Minneapolis: Lutheran University Press, 2004.

———. "Jesus Crucified and the Mission of the Church Within a Buddhist Context." In *Suffering and Redemption: Exploring Christian Witness within a Buddhist Context*, 39–77. Chicago: Division for Global Mission, 1998.

———. *Jesus, the Word, and the Way of the Cross: An Engagement with Muslims, Buddhists, Other Peoples of Faith*. Minneapolis: Lutheran University Press, 2008.

———. Review of *Scandalous God: The Use and Abuse of the Cross*, by Vitor Westhelle. *Word & World* 27/4 (2007) 456–66.

Tracy, David. *Dialogue With the Other: The Inter-Religious Dialogue*. Grand Rapids: Eerdmans, 1990.

———. "The Hidden God: The Divine Other of Liberation." *Cross Currents* 46/1 (1996) 5–16.
Trelstad, Marit A. Introduction of *Cross Examinations: Readings on the Meaning of the Cross Today*, 1–16. Minneapolis: Fortress, 2006.
Wengert, Timothy J. "'Peace, Peace . . . Cross, Cross' Reflections on How Martin Luther Related the Theology of the Cross to Suffering." *Theology Today* 59/2 (2002) 190–205.
Westhelle, Vitor. "The Church's Crucible: Koinonia and Cultural Transcendence." *Currents in Theology and Mission* 31/3 (2004) 211–18.
———. "Communication and the Transgression of Language in Martin Luther." *Lutheran Quarterly* 27 (2003) 1–27.
———. "The End of Christendom and Other Captivities: A Response to Douglas John Hall." *Currents in Theology and Mission* 22/6 (1995) 441–45.
———. "Idols and Demons: On Discerning the Spirits." *Dialog: A Journal of Theology* 41/1 (2002) 9–15.
———. "Luther on the Authority of Scripture." *Lutheran Quarterly* 19 (2005) 373–91.
———. "Proclamation and Obligation: On the Demonstration of the Spirit and of Power." *Word & World* 16/3 (1996) 328–39.
———. *The Scandalous God: The Use and Abuse of the Cross*. Minneapolis: Fortress, 2006.
———. "Scientific Sight and Embodied Knowledges: Social Circumstances in Science and Theology." *Modern Theology* 11/3 (1995) 341–61.
———. "Toward an Ethics of Knowledge." *Zygon* 39/2 (2004) 383–88.
———. "The Way the World Ends: An Essay on Cross and Eschatology." *Currents in Theology and Mission* 27/2 (2000) 85–97.
Williams, Delores S. "Black Women's Surrogacy Experience and the Christian Notion of Redemption." In *Cross Examinations: Readings on the Meaning of the Cross Today*, edited by Marit Trelstad. Minneapolis: Fortress, 2006.
Williams, Mark B. *Endo Shusaku: A Literature of Reconciliation*. New York: Routledge, 1999.
Wright, T. R. *Theology and Literature*. Boston: Blackwell, 1988.
Yagi, Seiichi. *Bukyo to kirisutokyo no setten* (*Contact of Point between Buddhism and Christianity*). Kyoto, Japan: Hozokan, 1975.
———. "Christ and Buddha." In *Asian Faces of Jesus*, edited by R. S. Sugirtharajah. Maryknoll, NY: Orbis, 1993.
———. "Ego and Self in New Testament and in Zen." In *Bible in a World Context: An Experience in Contextual Hermeneutics*, edited by Walter Dietrich and Ulrich Luz, 33–49. Grand Rapids: Eerdmans, 2002.
———. "Enlightenment and Liberation." *Journal of Asian American and Asian Theology* 4 (2001) 1–8.
———. "'I' in the Words of Jesus." In *The Myth of Christian Uniqueness*, edited by John Hick and Paul F. Knitter, 117–34. Maryknoll, NY: Orbis, 1987.
———. *Paul, Shinran, Jesus, and Zen*. Tokyo: Hozoukan, 1983.
———. *Shinran to Paul* (*Shinran and Paul*). Tokyo: Seidosha, 1989.
———. *Shinyaku Shisou no Kouzou* (*The Structure of the New Testament Thought*). Tokyo: Iwanami-shoten, 2002.
———. "Shinyaku Shisou ni-okeru Jita (*Self and Other in the New Testament*)" in *Isshinkyo to-wa Nanika* (*What is Monotheism?*) Tokyo: Tokyo University Press, 2006.

---. *Shinyaku Shisou no Seiritu* (*The Formation of the New Testament Thought*). Tokyo: Shinkyo shuppansha, 2003.
---. *Shukyo to Gengo* (*Religion and Language*). Tokyo: Nihon Kiristo-kyo, 1995.
---. "The Third Generation, 1945–1970." In *A History of Japanese Theology*, edited and translated by Furuya Yasuo, 83–111. Grand Rapids: Eerdmans, 1997.
---. "What Can Claim Absoluteness? The Uniqueness of Jesus and The Universality of the 'Self.'" *Journal of Asian American and Asian Theology* 1 (1996) 27–41.
Yagi, Seiichi, and Leonard Swidler. *A Bridge to Buddhist-Christian Dialogue*. New York: Paulist, 1990.

www.ingramcontent.com/pod-product-compliance
Lightning Source LLC
Chambersburg PA
CBHW051105160426
43193CB00010B/1319